ravage

(this place despite everything)

I'll not put this world on trial, even if it mistreats us.
I'll not put these times on trial, even if they are hustling us toward the fall.

I'll not put a system that attacks us on trial; I'll not put a religion that blinds us on trial; I'll not put an economy that assassinates, assaults, parches, smothers, pounds, and drowns us on trial.

I'll not put life on trial, despite its fundamental inadequacy, nor our species, which does not cease hating itself.
Besides, I'll launch no trial; the world has enough contrarians.
The best I can do is show that the hits have found their mark (and then).
So what can I do—one who does not share the confidence of troublemakers—to try to transmute what is real, attempt to rip up my own sinkholes, hold on to what is dying, flesh out time, hollow out impasses, and see sense appear, perhaps, in its shaky beat?

One day I chose to make a commitment to those places—in spite of everything—that are theatres, and I chose to linger in this one to invite dreamers and to dream with them,
to give more space to speech, more speech to speech.
I chose to write on a long wall with the title *I begin again* in order to recreate tirelessly and thus to converse endlessly with this world that never ceases to amaze me.

Take the word *ravage*, for example.
Still, yesterday, it inspired in me only fear and destruction, ugliness and chaos.
And then, one day, my country friend taught me that a ravage is also a place
where the deer gather to face the rigours of winter.

In winter, if you go for a walk in the forest, you might come upon a ravage, which you will recognize
by the disruption of the snow, by the many and mingled deer tracks,
like the imprint of mysterious writing, and you will see that the ravage is protected by tall evergreens that wrap their long, resinous arms around it.

The first time I saw a ravage I thought, "That's what we need! A spot to survive the winters, a place despite everything, a refuge for beauty, a stopping place for what hides itself! A ravage! A ravage! We need a ravage!"

I thanked my country friend and I returned to the city.
Ever since I begin again,
tirelessly.

And I hope, with you, to make a ravage from this theatre.

Ravage of Life

Evelyne de la Chenelière

translated by Louise H. Forsyth

Playwrights Canada Press

Toronto

Pour Louise H. Forsyth,
à qui nous devons tant

Meandering And Shakes

Part One: Writing On A Wall

> *I am wondering whether what we call poetry isn't in truth something which constantly inhabits, works and lies under written language so as to restore it to the ineffable from which it derives and toward which it keeps us moving.*
>
> —Giorgio Agamben, *Il fuoco e il racconto*

La vie utile had its first stage creation at Espace GO in Spring 2018 following a three-year residency that, without knowing it at first, would profoundly shake up my practice and the way I see writing.

As conceived by Artistic Director Ginette Noiseux, residencies at Espace GO are meant to nurture an ongoing dialogue between the theatre and an invited female artist. Over three seasons the resident artist is expected to initiate and inspire creations in mainstream programming while occupying a space alongside the regular season. The artist is encouraged to develop forms that reflect the questions she is exploring and her desires as an artist and to invite other artists to join her as appropriate. When this residency was offered to me my head began to spin as I looked at the range of possibilities. I had a premonition that it would be the site of an important inner conflict between *outside* and *inside*. Ironically, I was being invited to occupy a place at the same time I was wondering in what space I could best live.

Before making a commitment I felt it was important to look within myself for an approach that would allow me to enhance this residency but also remain tuned into my own deepest and most vital concerns. Above all, I had to find the drive, the surge of energy, since, I must admit, this invitation came at a moment when I was feeling great moral fatigue toward what is presently called *le métier* or, in more figurative terms, *le milieu*.[1]

How could I find the need for my work when the world is shrieking and tearing down a path to its own ruin? How could I still believe in the impact of art when no distinction is made between a poet and a publicist, between an evening of theatre and a restaurant outing? In the face of what seems to be a kind of censorship through excess, how could I hope to speak without having my words immediately deflated?

In her essay "The Cinema," Virginia Woolf stated, "People say that the savage no longer exists in us, that we are at the [tail] end of civilization, that everything has been said already, and that it is too late to be ambitious."[2] Despite the subtle and luscious irony in this sentence, I believe it evokes a painful feeling common to all generations since the beginning of time: the feeling of being born *too late*. However, this impression of an irreparable break between the self and the world has little to do with the period or the year of our birth; it comes, in my opinion, from a discrepancy

---

1 In playing with these two words that have similar sounds but diverging connotations, Evelyne de la Chenelière is making a point here about the troubled perspective on the theatre world she is developing throughout this essay and in *Ravage of Life*. *Métier* suggests fixed standards for professional competence, while *milieu* suggests what happens in a banal way in a general field. Both words risk stirring negative associations when they are meant to celebrate creativity, artistry, imagination, vision, spontaneity (LHF).

2 Virginia Woolf, "The Cinema," in *Selected Essays* (Oxford UP, 2008), 172.

between our interpretation of what is real and the ways by which it is presented to us from childhood.

That break, in the moment Ginette Noiseux made me the offer of becoming artist-in-residence, is what struck me as growing inexorably. So before accepting the invitation I launched into a process of reflection that took me to places I had been carefully avoiding—zones in which I was afraid of seeing my desire to write snuffed out forever. That's what was at stake: keeping alive an ever more precarious desire.

The kind of writing you see the most in public places, and particularly writing that takes shape on our stages, is often far from what I expect of it. The theatre has turned into a space akin to the courtroom, the pulpit, or the confessional. Scathing attacks are launched, accusations are thrown with a skill that disconcerts me, sermons are delivered in the name of virtues that bother me, endless and shameless admissions and confessions are made in a search for absolution that makes me uncomfortable. This grasp for backup is a symptom of our era feeling a lack of moral guarantees. What keeps us together in mediocrity and renunciation is a generalized fear of risk. The theatre has perhaps slowly fallen under the control of its subject, available for assimilation through affirmation—a *hygienic* art, a consumable, arrogant, conformist subversion, not to be discussed, which, contrary to what such subversion claims, feeds our denial.

What room is left for attention, anxiety, doubt, desire, ambiguity, mystery, opacity, uncertainty? Is there still a vacant space to commit to? Where? How? Why? For whom? Where is genuine resistance to be found? Is the theatre milieu bound to be a closed circle? Did I lose myself as a result of a lucky submission that gave me a place in this closed circle? Am I doomed to constantly fear the loss of the place that was made for me or that I took? Wouldn't it be better to endure a definitive rejection on the part of the milieu rather than trying desperately to fit into it just to keep myself alive there? Why do I find myself seeking an expulsion that would allow me no reinsertion, which would leave me no hope of an eventual reintegration? In fact, is it hope that renders us slaves to power? Should I give up hoping forever to become a pariah, finally disqualified for good? In short, finally free?

Sort of like when I was little and dreamt of having my place among the pretty girls, the ones who were feared, the desirable ones, the daunting ones in the schoolyard whose power I envied: I was ready for everything to win their favour, to have them reach their hand out to me and make me a place in their light. And yet, if I happened to win that place, I immediately felt unhappy because I knew that they could snatch it from me for no reason, with no explanation, and that place had a price: the price of my freedom. Is it necessary to be banned in order to be set free, to be able to see the possibility of something beyond? Is it necessary to be *outside*? And to what lengths am I ready to go to not be completely *inside*? To not adapt what I have to say to the flavour of the day? To not become a trendy artist? To not see my imagination channelled, captured in advance by what is more and more like the laws of supply and demand I have learned? To not be tempted to participate in the game of winners and conquerors, those celebrated by theatre, the pretty girls of the schoolyard, and to not become blind to the violence of this game? How does it happen that theatre, which from the start has been a place where the mechanics of domination are called into question, is participating today in the spread of the dogma of competition, in the struggle for power that it is seeking to resist? These are the questions, among others, that I tried to tie to my residency rather than running away from them.

Before I could accept the Espace GO offer, I had to find a way to throw myself into an action that was meaningful yet uncertain.

Into a place that would allow the unpredictable to bloom. For, in the state I found myself, I was no longer able to foresee anything. So I proposed to Ginette Noiseux that I undertake a work that would unfold throughout my entire residency. I presented my project in these terms:

I wish to deploy a slow and abundant artistic action.

I wish to give to the word residency its literal meaning by moving into the theatre as into an abode of writing.

I wish to displace the action of writing, to change axes and perspectives, to gain new freedoms.

I wish to explore ways to account for the transformation, erasure, and progression of writing, and to make visible the deletions, erasures, and corrections of this evolving writing.

I wish to engage in an action the exact meaning of which I am still unsure of and to be ready for a rush of meaning from the action.

I wish to write "transparently," on oversized, visible supports so that poetry blossoms in the building.

I wish to stain this place with words by giving a material and tangible dimension to the writing.

I wish what is written to be "iconized" thereby, the words referring as much to their mental image as to their acoustic and visual image.

I wish that this writing, having become the inscription of language usage, establish a relation between eternity (traces of writing) and the present moment (act of writing).

I wish that writing, having become handwriting, be tied to space, time, and duration.

Finally; I wish to resist the growing number of artistic events that call each time for promotion, profitability, and commentary by concentrating on a single evolving initiative.

I gave it the name of a writing worksite; my artistic residency dedicated to writing on a long wall that forms a place of passage and transition: the café-bar of Espace GO. Those three years of writing took the form of three layers, each one partially hiding the preceding one—like a palimpsest. The first year I produced an arrangement of words and collages on a wooden surface; the second year I carried the work on with a sheet of plexiglass placed a few centimetres from the wooden surface; finally, in the third year, on a sheet of stretched tulle I sewed shapes and words, completing the wall. Inspired by cocoons and chrysalides, this last layer was a way for me to put the two preceding layers into a latent state, all while making their potential felt. It seemed to me, while standing in front of the wall as a fixed image, it could create the sensation of being in front of multiple temporal realities: the past, peopled with icons and phantoms; the present, the perception of which is necessarily chaotic; and the future, a time of possibilities and of making.

I BEGIN AGAIN

On August 13, 2014, I picked up a paintbrush, dipped it into red paint, climbed up on a small ladder, and, on the white wall, traced letters that said, "Je recommence." Thus began my residency, with a move that resembled an interminable, unfinishable curve.

Beginning this wall terrified me; I could not bring myself to stain it with a mark that would represent the beginning of something. On the other hand, if the mark designated itself as a new beginning—that is to say, as participating in a vast thing already underway—I felt that I would suddenly be *capable* of writing. Yes, *beginning again* was acting in me like a driving force, a movement transformed into a goal, a guiding principle that would, without let-up, renew my urge to write by giving it infinite possibilities. At least I hoped so. And since those first traced letters, a strange work that I'm still trying to understand has taken shape.

What galvanized me in what became the title, *Je recommence*, is also its value as *foretold failure*—for I perceive the new beginning as a fundamental impossibility, an indecent promise. My use here of the word *recommencement* injects the notion of renewal into it, not simply of relapse. It is not just a matter of reiterating, but indeed of beginning again, of coming back to a state that preceded the habitual way of looking at things. In order to reach that fantastical idea of *re-commencement*, which requires a total reconfiguration of what is real, I projected myself into radical unlearning based on memory and forgetting, as if recasting my imaginary had first to pass through the reactivation, then the reaffirmation of our collective memory, transmitted through time. So I chose two formative books, builders of my imaginary and my relation to the real, which would become the main sources of my exploration of a buried memory: the Bible and the *Précis de grammaire française*.[3]

3 Maurice Grévisse, a Belgian teacher and grammarian, published the first edition of *Précis de grammaire française* in 1939, following his *Le bon usage* (1936). Both have been through a number of editions and have retained their primary status as authorities in matter of French grammar and usage. They are widely used throughout educational establishments in France and in the francophone world (LHF).

Why The Bible?

Whether or not one practises a religion—whether one is of such and such a faith—our religious heritage is weighty and determining. The fate of our soul and its salvation weigh like a mute curse on all minds. We have been bearing for millennia processions of images that can essentially be divided into two poles: the terrifying ones—cadavers, exploded or swollen bodies devoured by animals or gnawed by flames—and the sublime ones promising peace, bliss, ecstasy.

Perhaps these poles act like unconscious landmarks, making it possible for us to tolerate the intolerable in reality, to live while knowing the ordinary horror of our world of the living, to not go mad at the sight of murderous images coming at us from everywhere, to deceive ourselves by dreaming of violence as the fruit of outside events when it is a part of us. The images situated between these two poles constitute a sort of void, leaving few imprints in our collective imagination. Paradoxically, it is a saturated void, a *full hollow*.

What I am interested in exploring with writing is this break in extreme images, this place that we inhabit of iconic compromise between the sight of our own decomposition and the ecstatic contemplation promised us by religion. But how do I enter this place, that of our terrestrial existence, between what we are loath to imagine and what we scarcely dare dream of? My work wants to envision that place differently, reread it, reinvent it, renew representations of it—*begin it again* [*le recommencer*].

Why French Grammar?

An extraction, accidental or intentional, often serves as the starting point for the state of reinvention I'm trying to accede to, or, as Bernard-Marie Koltès expresses it, for a "perfect comprehension" of the world that would precede everything learned, including—and perhaps especially—language. As if language had the defect, in giving meaning to the world, of justifying the unjustifiable, of naming the unnameable: "It is a matter of finding once again first faculties of perception, that much deeper since they are first. It is a matter of seeking perfect comprehension, that is comprehension that knows nothing of exegesis and justification."[4] Exile would be a necessary condition for our "first faculties of perception," extraction, and flight as an active opposition to the status quo and inertia, meandering taken on like a project, making it possible for us to leave a known territory familiar to the point of blindness.

I applied this notion of exile doubly on my wall of writing. First, I left a sort of native land, the place where I have been writing since childhood: the piece of paper. I extracted myself from that paper

4 Bernard-Marie Koltès, *Les amertumes* (Éditions de Minuit, 1998), 10. Translation by Louise H. Forsyth.

where I was born as a writer in the hope of renewing the gaze I cast on the world, and in so doing extract my way of responding to it in writing. Without leaving Montréal, my place of writing became unknown to me. I also wanted to exile myself from my own language by beginning with the principle that the first language not only designates the real, but moulds it and seals it. So I sought to claim it as a foreign language, even if that meant simply changing my relationship with the handwriting of my mother tongue through rediscovering the designs traced by writing it.

WRITING IN FULL FORCE

At the theatre entrance, as a way of introducing my project that was taking shape, I placed these words:

> *Not so long ago, a small two-year-old boy stirred a very strong emotion in me. He was telling me something. I don't remember the content of what he had to say, but I shall remember all my life his commitment to using language.*
>
> *I remember thinking, while he was catching his breath, he is speaking with his full force.*
>
> *It wasn't just the volume of his voice that was strong (the maximum of what his breath and vocal cords allowed, it seemed to me), it was the force of his body fully invested in the effort to speak; it was a boundless vital force; it was the energy exerted to find the word that would make of him a heeded and understood being; it was like a hand extended by the tongue; it was the difficult search for the road, that mental path of the combatant that ties the desire to the concept, the concept to the word, the word to the sentence, the sentence to its expression.*

Each fragment he spoke was a draft, a trial, the opposite of despair. Every part of his being seemed to be called into making possible the full, vibrant, dazzling word he was speaking.

I have the desire to be like this little boy.

I have the desire to write with my full force.

The physical commitment required for the action of writing on a wall was a way for me to make the meaning of my commitment to creation visible and tangible. I felt that I was *writing writing*—that is to say tracing it, painting it, sticking it, making it material, indeed, an excess transcending thought itself.

Writing while standing, lying down, perching, taking the chance that a body invested in writing can rip language right out of its own system of alienation, trivialization, subjection. As if only the body could restore the strangeness of words, separate them from every value established by verbal habits. In that way writing became almost a dance, a suite of codified rhythmic gestures making sense beyond reason.

Writing *with the body* in the same way you make the sign of the cross: as you become aware of your forehead, your heart, your shoulders, from left to right—and of their obvious symmetry. Perhaps, in the final analysis, of the irruption of the divine into humanity's history.

DESIRE AND REMORSE

Right from the start this project also entailed the desire to explore and bring to light a sort of *pre-form* preceding the final, completed, *presentable* work. Displayed in such a way on a wall, writing can demonstrate the transformation, erasure, progression of a creative act so that the deletions, mistakes, corrections appear. In short, what usually remains hidden from readers and spectators. So I worked at making concrete the babble of a *will* to write through an extension—or a continuous reiteration—of the impulse driving it.

I had the feeling at the sight of this work of digging into trembling form, its infinite potential, its readiness. The tension of writing, formed by a constant struggle between desire and remorse, between *inside* and *outside*, was to be rendered visible, almost tangible, in the same way that can be done with repentance in painting. Thus, in the course of days and layers, to the beat of my thrusts and retractions, the palimpsest wall became the palpitating, unstated, and dogged embryo of a thing that, still today, I don't know what it was.

WANDER LINES

While I was writing I remembered an exhibition I had seen in Paris at the Palais de Tokyo in 2012 that had really struck me. Entitled *Cartes et lignes d'erre*, it spoke of an experiment carried out over ten years by Fernand Deligny, a French educator who became a writer and filmmaker. He dedicated himself to the search for a *possible* way of life for autistic children and for a way to connect with them without recourse to a language—that is, ours—that does not speak to them.

The exhibition was a collection of maps representing on the same territory the daily wanderings of these children, superimposed on those of adults. Deligny named the drawings *lignes d'erre* [wander lines], his experiment being based on the intuition that such tracings would constitute a way into the world of children held outside our language.

Retaining an imperishable memory of these drawings I had found magnificent, powerful and, in particular, alive—and persuaded that my writing workshop, in certain places, was a response to the lines and forms that had saturated my memory—I acquired the catalogue five years later. The psychoanalyst Bertrand Ogilvie noted in his afterword for the work that "as by a sort of invitation or choreographic provocation, these trails and these moves, these comings and goings gradually have joined together so that, at unpredictable points, common dances appear, simultaneously trivial and sublime, bound around life's most indispensable and elementary gestures."[5]

I realized that I too am seeking, in my way, a form of writing that is not subject to the authority of language and words. We are conditioned, educated, taught to envisage life through words; words are often our only recourse for making sense of things, sense of the ties that bind us, sense of transiency, suffering, death. And what if the problem was precisely sense itself—sense we try to detect in everything and everywhere we cast our eyes? What if, rather than trying to inject sense—that is to say: our *idea* of sense—into life, we worked at better experiencing its pulse, vibration, movements, and breaths as well as all its manifestations? Would our art not effectively find itself more *alive*? If I was writing on this wall, it was to push the reflex that attaches me to the sense of words out of the way, to make the life carried by words burst forth.

5 Bertrand Ogilvie, "Postface," in *Cartes et lignes d'erre/Maps and Wander Lines: Traces du réseau de Fernand Deligny, 1969–1979*, edited by Sandra Alvarez de Toledo (L'Arachnéen, 2013), 399. Translation by Louise H. Forsyth.

IT'S JUST A WALL

I suspected, since statistics, noise, and glamour are celebrated these days, that I would need great power of concentration and a good deal of faith to keep alive the desire of this action, *writing on a wall*, and attributing it, over the length of its creation, the same significance I found in it at the start.

What I had not foreseen, what I could not have predicted, is the point at which this slowly unfolding writing, this wall to which I returned almost daily, was going to provoke such varied and contradictory reactions. My work, if it stirred curiosity, interest, enthusiasm, and even excitement, also ran into consternation, indifference, derision, and much silence. Certain remarks, although made in all innocence, appeared particularly violent to me: "It's so cute, your wall!"; "You're still here?!"; "Oh, you're making your little collages . . . "; "Excuse me, where are the washrooms?"

Suddenly my project transformed into a rampart of insurmountable incomprehension between me and others. As a result I had to struggle against the feeling of emptiness that was invading me. My great—and constant—vulnerability when it comes to this wall can undoubtedly be explained by the fact that a change took place—almost a reversal—in the place it occupied in me. At the start, I conceived it as a *parallel* adventure, in the margin of my *principal* works that were easier to grasp, being pieces that entailed deadlines and remuneration. Slowly, almost surreptitiously, the wall became the heart of my practice and my reflection on creation, the starting point for all that stirred my spirit. This field of exploration began to take up more space, to project onto the whole of what I was working on elsewhere. In other words, I was fashioning a piece that, far beyond my expectations, was conditioning me in return. Yes, the more I committed to this action the more it became vital to me, the more I attached myself frankly to the uncertainty and the instability of its sense—or, rather, of its vitality—just as to the countless ways in which it can be approached.

Then one evening there was a charity event. I had spent part of the day cutting out and gluing birds. I had not *produced* any text, but I had the feeling that my birds said a lot: seen from a distance, they turned the transparent surface white and rendered it vibrant. The quick identification of currents was possible, several flights emerging from a common direction; when you got close to the wall, you discovered that its apparent whiteness came in fact from an amalgam of beige, grey, blond, and pink; if you lingered a bit, you noticed birds of impossible shape, certain of them deformed to the point of resembling creatures borrowed from a prehistoric imaginary, animals emerging from the marine depths at the beginning of time. The collage was an interrogation of notions of appearance and representation.

Even if this kind of event invariably represents a challenge for me—I have a lot of difficulty with noisy places, and I always feel inadequate in starting or sustaining an interesting conversation—I arrived at the charity event in very good spirits, with the feeling of having accomplished something, of having *done good work*. And that was where I ran into a vivacious young woman with whom I quickly felt myself at ease. She had a winning smile and didn't fail to impress me because she was very sure of herself without being arrogant for all that—my dream! Attractive and sunny, this patron, who works in a lawyer's office, loves the theatre. I experienced a sincere pleasure listening to her, even feeling a bit ashamed, for she had succeeded in just ten minutes and without artifice in bringing down my worst prejudices where benefit evenings are concerned, those forced marriages between artists and businesspeople.

It was then that she asked me a question that made my mouth drop and has haunted me ever since: "And what is *your* ambition?" I know there was no malice in this nor innuendo, and yet, these words came to me like a slap. I smiled and, to give myself some time, I congratulated the patron for asking a very good question. I felt ridiculous and, without giving an answer, I stammered out a few words about the notion of ambition before finding an excuse to politely slip away. I spent the rest of the evening mauling my plastic glass without ever engaging in conversation with anyone for fear of bursting into sobs, with that voice in my head repeating: "You have no ambition."

The next day I tried to get rid of those hurtful words, but they kept coming back, forcing me to deal seriously with the question to keep it from becoming a hindrance to my work. Cruel thoughts tortured me: "I have never thought about ambition. I have never drawn up a plan nor set a goal. I act by instinct, like an animal. My lack of ambition will leave me forever mediocre. Besides, my artistic approach is clearly without scope, desperately local. I was born in Montréal and here I am, forty years later, writing on the wall of a Montréal theatre, for a band of illiterates and the culturally backward"—once again, my pathetic opinion of myself showed itself taking the form of scorn for others.

I remained stunned for several days out of deep regret for being an artist without ambition, limited, incapable of projecting myself into the future, and no longer finding any interest in the journey that had led me to want to write on a wall. I began a search for the ambitions of artists and writers who know how to dream. Then I discovered that my ambition was not linked to power. On the contrary, the force to which I aspire finds its origin in powerlessness. The very principle of getting to the top leaves me cold. I do not envisage ambition as a movement upward, in the way you climb a ladder. The only verticality that concerns me is the one that leads me into depths. Transcendence, as I imagine it, is what directs us toward the hollow, the buried, the gut, the fire. Toward the origin.

One day I was told that my writing was anachronistic. I think that person was trying to get to me. Well, the idea pleased me a lot. The thing is that I love the irrelevance of fossils and of what survives from the past; everywhere I cast my eyes I see precedence, see our stubborn rituals and our unshakable beliefs, our mad desire for the other, our unheard-of capacity to hate that person.

I am interested in what stubbornly returns and has always done so. The history that speaks to me is primitive, of which neither the beginning nor the end can be known. And that's how I see us, struggling for an incomprehensible and variable length of time between what was not the beginning and what will not be the end. So I often wonder, what is our time and what is our present? What to do with it? Does it require an answer? Must we run away from it? Must we pull ourselves out of it? Must we dive in? Must we open our eyes, or, on the contrary, close them? How much time?

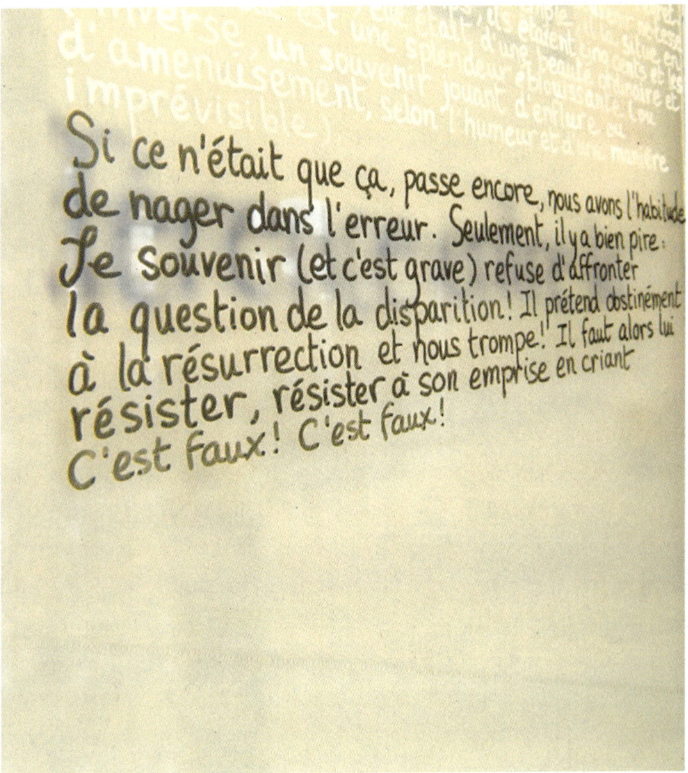

THE WOMB OF THE WALL

I know nothing of nostalgia, but I love *the before*.

I love bulbs, shoots, buds, eggs, partially opened fruit, swollen bellies; I love whatever contains the embryo of an unknown thing; I love soft envelopes or shells, fine membranes, sometimes translucid, that make you suspect the breathing and trembling of something inside, a thing in the process of becoming, uncertain, a thing before something more presentable, before clear contours, before fur, plumage, colour, style. I adore thinking: What is going to come out from this belly, this garden, this spawning area? I love it when dancers mark their movements without actually doing them, totally wrapped in the thrust and the memory, anticipating a fullness to come—or not. I love the taut bow, the tension before the leap, the hovering before the drop, the inhalation before the breath or the note. I also love the obvious retraction. I love seeing the traces of what *could have* emerged but was rejected—like cuttings in the days of film. I love it when artists give themselves, in full view, the right to contradict themselves, to revoke a part of their creation, without judging it or hiding it like an unworthy or shameful thing.

That's what, among other things, I wanted to write about with my palimpsest wall: what could happen, flourish, ripen, or dry up before seeing the light of day. Because certain fruits die and fall without having become swollen and for which only picking remains; nature makes no fuss about them and begins again.

So my ambition would be intimately linked to the tenacity as well as the spasmodic and muscular relationship I maintain with writing. Since writing for me—contrary to what is sometimes said about it—does not *flow*: it surges forth with effort, enjoys no gravity; on the contrary, writing opens a road for itself against all laws, including that of gravity. No, writing does not flow; it climbs while it digs.

My action was one of patience and, as I like to believe, of resistance. Even subtle, even oblique, even without scandalizing, this resistance that never stops driving me is very real.

At the start of my residency, I resisted the satisfaction of *having written*, prolonging instead the discomfort and the solitude of writing in the *present.* I resisted the cadence encouraged and validated nowadays in art and literature. Today, everything is set up so that artists and writers find sense and justification for their work through abundance and flamboyance. You have to produce a lot—and make noise—you have to engender shapes that are clearly identifiable and, it must be said, encourage consumption, that stir immediate approval in spectators, readers, and medias who will then *answer the call.*

I chose, in dedicating myself to this wall, to celebrate patient resistance—or resistant patience—resistance that I seek in myself and that I call for at the same time in readers-spectators so that they find, slowly, heeding their own beat, the life beneath this fabrication, beneath this revelation, beneath this *waste of time*—that is, beneath this time stolen from productivity. Yes, in view of the frenzy of creation, in view of the avalanche of strident ideas offered to us, in view of the frantic rate in which new works are being signed, how can I still dare to write? By way of response to the abundance, I said to myself, I might as well exceed the demand, create what no one expects nor is asking for: a writing worksite on a wall. Writing in the hope of grace and chance and *inscribing* this writing by rendering obstinately visible the repeated attempt at reaching out to life.

By physically extending the time of impulse and readiness, the time of uncertainty and failure, I came to see a form of writing that was material and throbbing—in the sense that one's flesh throbs—the potential for which seemed as vast to me as its inadequacy; those words and those tracings that filled the wall were in the image of the world as I represent it to myself: partially legible, unstable, vibrant. That is where emergence and disappearance succeed each other so quickly that they get mixed up together.

On the wall motifs forged their way slowly; certain words leapt into view like striking testimonials in their colour, proof of a vitality inherent to matter. And this palimpsest appeared to me to become radiant to the point of bursting out of its own frame, as if it were claiming an existence beyond the wall.

OF AND FROM THE PLACE OF WRITING

Still on the wall:

> *. . . I am writing to you that what I would like more than anything in the world is to know how to carve stone, so as to inscribe separate little letters, perhaps on the facade of a church no one wants anymore; yes, if I was writing while carving stone, writing would be the encounter of flesh and mineral, writing would be a way of bringing together the age of speech and the age of stone, writing would be a dangerous action, you understand, because of the mallet and chisel, and writing would become a material form that can be touched, in relief; I could even perhaps write in braille and be happy thinking that people will have to caress my writing in order to read it, and perhaps, finally, I would no longer say to myself on condition they like me on condition they like me, from the scaffolding where I would see the world from then on, and I would believe myself out of reach, protected from its stings, and I would live that way, perched, on a real worksite, a writing worksite that would resemble a hanging garden, from which I would write in a solitary and populated language,*

> *that is how I dream myself, like a heroine of solitude and freedom, an anachronistic and exiled heroine, without a name to call her for no one thinks of speaking to her, a heroine who mixes her dust with that of the stones while musing that humans and stones belong to the same immense oblivion, and that this is a good thing, yes, if I can I shall become that heroine, a heroine whose language and tongue*[6] *serve nothing and no one, whose language and tongue do not serve, whose language patiently makes its little strokes of tongue, and then, in all the time remaining to me, I'll spend it writing, day after day after day, my language and tongue will carve little breaches in the stone walls in an attempt to make them speak.*

Following such an outburst of writing, I wondered where this fantasy of carving stone came from, as if this action represented an *overwriting*, indeed a writing that would have enhanced existence. And I thought of a passage from *The Hunchback of Notre-Dame* that had struck me: "This will kill that." This is a statement Victor Hugo has one of his characters make, a character who dreads the invention of the printing press:

> Now, what a precarious immortality is that of the manuscript! How much more solid, durable, unyielding, is a book of stone! In order to destroy the written word, a torch and a Turk are sufficient. To demolish the constructed word, a social revolution, a terrestrial revolution are required. The barbarians passed over the Colosseum; the deluge, perhaps, passed over the Pyramids.
>
> In the fifteenth century everything changes.

6 In French, "tongue" and "language" are the same word (*langue*) (LHF)..

> Human thought discovers a mode of perpetuating itself, not only more durable and more resisting than architecture, but still more simple and easy. Architecture is dethroned. Gutenberg's letters of lead are about to supersede Orpheus's letters of stone.
>
> *The book is about to kill the edifice.*[7]
>
> [. . .] The grand poem, the grand edifice, the grand work of humanity will no longer be built: it will be printed.[8]

I remember that, since reading this, I have never looked at a building in the same way. And I believe that my desire to inscribe writing on a wall had its source, among others, in Hugo's reflection: What *place* of writing guarantees that its ideas will endure, be imperishable, indestructible, thereby eternal? It seems that I deliberately chose to act in opposition to progress, in opposition to the infinite spread of thought made possible by printing and, a bit more recently, by computing. Perhaps when it gets right down to it, I was looking for the place of writing where the intrinsic paradox of the action itself is found, the action that makes a mark but knows everything is destined to disappearance and oblivion.

In effect, the wall has been demolished; this was foreseen; it was not made to last. A small part of me, despite everything, likes to believe that something could remain, a thing that would be neither book nor building, but instead a kind of living radiation pursuing an unfathomable and invisible trajectory.

---

7 Italics are in the original.

8 Victor Hugo, *Notre-Dame de Paris*, translated by Isabel Florence Hapgood (Project Gutenberg, 2001), https://www.gutenberg.org/cache/epub/2610/pg2610-images.html.

Je me suis donc engagée dans le recommencement, dans l'inachevable, dans une tentative insensée de rétablir le monde par-dessus le monde, comme si le monde était un mur qui demande congé de sa réalité. Parce que, vouloir écrire le monde, le mettre en mots, c'est peut-être justement lui donner congé de tout le reste. Et je me demande alors : Mais l'écriture, elle, de quoi peut-elle prendre congé ? Peut-on libérer l'écriture d'elle-même ? Peut-être un texte débarrassé de sa grammaire, des mots exemptés de leur réseau de relations, jusqu'à ce qu'il ne reste qu'une liste du monde, qu'un inventaire, qu'un répertoire subjectif et poétique. Car quelle écriture peut rendre compte de l'hébétude, de la sidération, si ce n'est une écriture syncopée, rompue, amputée de ses marqueurs de relation ? Parce que, il faut l'admettre, c'est un aveu et j'en ai honte, je suis rarement indignée, je suis rarement scandalisée, contrairement à ce qu'il faudrait, je reste, la plupart du temps, hébétée. J'ai beau appeler de toute mon âme l'état d'indignation, cet état qui semble la seule bonne réponse devant le spectacle du monde, je demeure pour ainsi dire bloquée à l'état d'hébétude, dans une sorte de sidération perpétuelle, et depuis toujours, d'ailleurs, enfant, ma bouche demeurait toujours ouverte, ma mère me disait ferme un peu ta bouche quand tu ne parles pas, ça donne l'air abruti de garder la bouche ouverte, et j'ai appris à fermer ma bouche, à pincer mes lèvres et à bloquer ma mâchoire, mais il m'arrive encore d'oublier

WRITING FREELY

If I were to summarize what went into the project, the intention, the source of this long creation, I would say that it was above all a desire for freedom, a concept upon which I shall never stop reflecting. Freedom in art cannot, *ought* not, be confused with the right or permission to create without fear of reprisal, nor with the means (technical, financial) to create. Even if these conditions are indispensable for the activity of an artist or writer, they do not in themselves guarantee freedom—which is an effort of thought to which the creator must incessantly return.

For thinking freely is a demanding exercise. In order to aspire to it, one must first have a sense of belonging in a place, a period, and a culture that condition in large part one's way of seeing the world. Despite any individuation process, even with the certainty of one's non-adherence to the realm, the cost of striving for freedom is a painful and repeated exclusion from everything that is familiar, reassuring, and attractive to us. This is to say even in the tranquility of a *room of one's own*, to adopt once again Virginia Woolf's famous expression, that creating freely is work to be done every day and a vow to be renewed from hour to hour.

There is another factor that must be added to that: in creation, the freedom of a work is not only the extension of its author's free spirit. It derives as well from the responsibility of those who receive the literary or artistic work. According to this principle, creating freely is vain, indeed impossible, if one is not read and interpreted freely. That is to say, from a point of view detached from all simplistic a priori views—those in particular held by critics, the first official interpreters of art who give a sort of indelible reference point to the work.

Women, too often, are read very poorly; they see the body of their work reduced to their personality, to their condition, as if it were difficult to admit that women give shape and order to material that is more vast than their selves. Their pen, when it has no response other than silence or indifference, is immediately *tamed* by the discourse that tries to define it. Whether it is the fruit of conditioning or clearly a manifestation of bad faith, this discourse sustains us in an interpretive error by preventing—or, at the very least, by reducing—the universal scope and critical force of women's words. In that way, even if no one dares express it anymore, this idea continues to act like a poison in our collective unconscious and perverts the way creations by women are seen: a woman speaks to women, while a man speaks to humanity.

If women, in our so-called progressive societies, are no longer reduced to silence, they are still reduced—or, rather, restricted—to the domain of the intimate and experiential, a place of feeling and memory. There are few intellectuals and critics, men or women, who welcome women onto erotic, theoretical, or philosophical territory without automatically confining their work to the expression of a feminist or feminine stand. This inevitably reflects onto the perception of women's creativity generally, but especially in condemning what women have to say, most often, to be toothless.

Creative people define their identity over time as much by their work, their personal research, and their stand as by the reception of their work. The painter Anselm Kiefer states, "It is you who decide what the paintings are and what I am."[9] In other words, it will not be enough for women to free themselves from what stands in the way of their thinking freely, perceiving themselves freely, dreaming themselves freely in order to be truly free. It would be equally necessary that views of their work and discussion around it be just as free.

I'm not denying here my belonging to the vast movement of women's writing. In fact I willingly claim it—on condition that such

---

9 Anselm Kiefer, quoted by Daniel Arasse, *Anselm Kiefer* (Éditions du Regard, 2012), 88. Translation by Louise H. Forsyth.

belonging is not exclusive, nor that it is the only or systematic way into what I write. In this sense I'm not claiming anything excessive, only a *just* look—I use this word to speak as much of correctness as of justice—cast on what women create: may the work of every woman be seen and read as it truly is, and not as one would like it to be.

This reminds me of the *glass ceiling*, which designates that invisible limit standing in the way of women coming to power and into decision-making positions. I don't doubt its existence, including in the field of arts and letters, but what I sense even more strongly is another kind of obstacle: I imagine it like a frosted window between the works of women and the rest of the world, with a crust of rime obstructing the view. This fine layer of ice forms so slowly that it is not even noticed. It is simply that the frosted window makes us see a blurry landscape.

Ever since I wrote in red letters "Je recommence," I have been wondering whether there is not also in that declaration, buried somewhere, the desire to repeat differently, to re-speak—as when you wish to be better understood, as if there had been a misunderstanding. This word, *malentendu*, fascinates me: a priori, what is defined as an error in interpretation refers back to hearing, since it is about a thing that has been *mal entendue* [poorly heard, poorly understood], and yet we seek to *clear up* or dissipate a misunderstanding, as if it was about a problem of vision, of a fog that must be cleared in order to see clearly.

THINGS AREN'T ALL THAT CLEAR

It's only now that I become aware of the scope of the subtitle that I put in parentheses after "Je recommence," "(tout n'est pas si clair)," at the time I wrote my first words on the wall. I have been asking myself ever since what I meant by that statement, what sense did I give it at the time of writing: what is *not so clear*? Is it I who have not been clear? Do I need to start over differently? Or then again, is it about that frosted window I've been talking about, a window through which I am read as all women are read, that makes me claim clarity? Where will full clarity come from? Where will full light come from?

Today, when I think back to the wall, I remember that it was carpeted with eyes: open eyelids, closed, torn, cut out, trembling eyelids sheltering dreams, or eyelids ever open on prying eyes. There was also the eye of God pursuing Cain right into his tomb, a girl's eyes no longer knowing how to close, the eyes of the severed head of Orpheus, closed forever. The wall was an assortment of gazes. It ended with these sentences:

> *To find rest from the sight of the world, you must close your eyes.*
>
> *Sweet dreams. You must dream now. It might not bring you rest.*

That assumes that you never know when you see best, eyes open or closed. Maybe we need to have "les yeux clos écarquillés" [eyes wide shut] to use Samuel Beckett's expression in *Cap au pire*,[10] and admit that we will always be forced to grope for our way as we walk in an endless night, sometimes in mud, always in the dark.

---

10 *Cap au pire* is a novella by Samuel Beckett, first appearing in 1983 in English as *Worstward Ho*. Samuel Beckett, *Cap au pire* (Éditions de Minuit, 1991), 12. Translation by Édith Fournier.

FENÊTRE

Interval

The start of my writing on the wall corresponded to the moment when walking became practically the only way I got around Montréal. I have always liked walking, but, until a few years ago, I thought that leaving point A and getting to point B was like passing the landmarks of lost time. The nature of my work means that sometimes I have to go to several neighbourhoods in the same day. I had opted in favour of the car or public transportation, depending upon what seemed the most efficient to me, the aim being to take a minimum amount of time to reach the destination and, ultimately, to return home as early as possible. I also tried the bicycle when enthusiasts convinced me it would be even faster. Well, after several horrible accidents where cyclists lost their lives or were seriously injured, I gave up forever on the bike in the city. Getting around represented intervals in my eyes, both non-time and non-place transitory spaces from which I always projected myself toward a destination, arrival, elsewhere, right spot, momentarily set somewhere, *in my right place.*

One day—and I haven't yet completely recovered from it—I realized that it had become useless, indeed senseless, to hurry in order to get home after a day's work. I had to accept the fact that there was no longer any child waiting impatiently for my return. My partner's sons no longer lived with us. They began their lives as young adults in an apartment. Our daughters were students and hadn't needed assistance with their homework or lessons for a long time. I thought that my presence when they came home from school meant something reassuring, stabilizing, and secretly I felt good about *being there*, quite ready to hear the account of their day, to receive their secrets, to support them, console them if called for. But my daughters are not *waiting* for me. When I opened the door, always more or less out of breath, they were polite and greeted me, but were not anxious for a conversation with me before dinner, the time when they came down from their room . . . only to go back up as soon as the table was cleared. Not only did I have the feeling that my daughters didn't need me to be there to welcome them, but I believe, on the contrary, that they appreciated my absence, which gave them some solitude, a kind of buffer between their social life and their family life.

Further to this acknowledgement, I stopped rushing home. I began to move around solely by walking. My entire relation to time was transformed by this. I enjoyed prolonging the transition and engaging with this space-time rather than perpetually living with somewhere else in mind.

It is not rare for me to walk several hours a day. And I keep trying to understand through what miracle this gives me the impression of *having more time*. I must insist here that I take no *athletic* pride in this new habit. It's not about a physical challenge, nor an ecological stance, or a firm principle, but perhaps, more simply—and more mysteriously—a sort of hope of discovering a space-time where the part of myself that cannot exist elsewhere might engage. When it comes right down to it, displacement, a sort of place without contours, might be successful in making me see the world I live in otherwise—I who have the impression of walking in a fog.

In fact, I have always had the feeling of getting close to what is real through my ears. I have very good hearing, to the point of being intolerant of certain noises that bother no one else but me. I have often wondered if the fact of hearing excessively didn't render me blind. I have no photographic memory, no sense of direction. I don't notice if a certain piece of furniture has been moved, if a certain person has gained or lost weight. I'm incapable of guessing the age of someone. I never recognize the face of those who have been introduced to me fewer than ten times. I have to have *heard* them for them to come back to mind. Only the intonation of their voice makes a powerful impression in my memory. While I was walking, I noticed that I was starting, gradually, to see better. And I wanted what I had never wanted before: to draw what I remembered after my walk, or yet again, the images that had suddenly grabbed me. I don't know yet what that means.

I have the impression that walking prolongs the interval by giving it the value of an irreplaceable, autonomous, full instant. It is no longer about a distance to cover or to abolish, but a space to get into through movement and which alters your senses, as if the receptors themselves found themselves modified by the displacement. Then I see something other than what looking brings to me; *seeing* is no longer simply the approximate result of images unconsciously identified, classified, prioritized, but maybe, instead, a *timeless* vision, a vision stirred by the feeling of belonging entirely to this world, as it always has been, as it is, and as it will become.

On first sight, what is called *urban fauna* knows what it's doing. People who walk have a manner, a direction. That's why discontinuous, jerky, hesitant, or erratic steps are immediately noticed, causing us to take a small detour—so as to not follow in the steps of madness or despair. In these missteps, often seen in men and women intoxicated by drugs or alcohol and who find themselves most of the time in great moral, physical, and economic misery, I read the visible signs of distress, suffering, anger, fatigue, idleness, lack, a terrible and almost unimaginable lack. Simply by walking these men and these women take on the vagrant in each of us, the part of us that is lame, that limps, is broken, poverty-stricken. I have seen that only while walking.

Part Two: Toward *Ravage of Life*

Open up signs, try to eviscerate theatre. Make theatre the place where thought finds its body. Dig into the space that exists between the parts of a sentence. Believe in the defeat of the story that also brings about its reversal and its rebirth. Free oneself from a grammar that binds like a spell, that inhibits the will to think. Remember the words of Ludwig Wittgenstein: "*The limits of my language* mean the limits of my world."

INDUCE WRITING

A fundamental part of my residency, despite the fact that it was based on intimate and solitary action, was the invitation that I in turn extended to artists to create an object that would, moved by the wall, enter into dialogue with it. In that way, autonomous forms were produced, each one of which represented, for me, the meeting place between creators' personal paths and the way in which my writing project worked for them. The objects, which can be described as *satellite-like*, derive from different artistic practices, different creative languages, different sensitivities.[11]

In *The Rustle of Language*, Roland Barthes writes that

11 David Ospina, Daniel Canty, Dany Boudreault, James Hyndman, Julie Le Breton, Christiane Pasquier, Julien Éclancher, Marlène Gélineau Payette, Max-Otto Fauteux, Justin Laramée, Olivia Boudreau, Morena Prats, and, finally, Marie Brassard are, in that order, the artists whose contributions I solicited (EdlC).

> The Text stands in the way of cultural typology's game coming into play: showing the *limitless* nature of a work means turning it into a Text; even if reflection on the Text starts with literature (that is, an object formed by the institution), the Text necessarily does not stop there; wherever a signifying activity is staged in accordance with the rules of combination, transformation and displacement, there is Text; in written creations, of course, but also in the play of images, signs and objects: in films, in animations, in ritual objects.[12]

The Text, once you agree with this comprehensive definition, designates much more than written production. As I see it, it draws its most vast and thrilling meaning, the making of a world covering the world, through a way of looking that is personal, curious, and engaged in a story that precedes it. In accordance with this principle, the artists who worked within the frame of my invitation, whatever their medium or their language, created Text, fruit of their intimate and secret relation with the wall; thanks to their ways of seeing that convert reality, ways of seeing that are fertile and inspired looking at the wall, they pulverized it, made it burst open, gutted it, unfolded it infinitely to the point where it opens beyond itself. A bird overreaching its own wingspan.

---

12 Roland Barthes, « Jeunes chercheurs, » in *Le bruissement de la langue: Essais critiques IV* (Éditions du Seuil, 1984), 102. Translation by Louise H. Forsyth.

FROM THE WALL TO THE STAGE

The last artist I invited was Marie Brassard. I asked her to be the director of the show that was to close my residency, since I have always seen in her a kind of double. If I am a writer *for* the stage, she is a writer *of* the stage; I was convinced that the intermingling of what we wrote would bring a surprising, free, and unusual work. In particular, I knew that the undertaking led by Marie would be a rich and profound human adventure, a thousand leagues removed from considerations aimed at success—which mean nothing to me.

We quickly agreed on our working method. Or rather I should say it was barely mentioned, since we are, the one like the other, artists essentially carried along by faith in intuition, in meandering, in the richness of the unconscious and the accidental, as well as in the unfathomable mystery when the right form appears.

We drew our inspiration from the Espace GO café-bar wall, pulling out motifs, themes, possible characters, but also grasping what it said to us beyond words. We discussed, wandered, looked at films, talks, documentaries; we exchanged books; while I was writing bits of text that we were reading, it came to us little by little that I should compose infinitely flexible material so as to nourish an open and mobile form, just like the wall in which it was finding its source. It mattered to us to bring to light the limitless nature of what we can see and understand in that which surrounds us, contains us, maintains us, survives us.

How do we read the world before we have learned to speak? Is there a form other than language to embrace the limitlessness of living thought? How is it possible for time to unfold differently on stage? How can the stage be turned into a territory where nothing sets or becomes immobile, and where each step, gesture, wave,

regard

and shock modifies its contours? How can the stage suggest a place beyond place, out of frame, beyond norm and beyond time, a place where, simply, something is taking shape?

THE DEAD AND THE LIVING

With the aim of giving shape to this space-time poetics, I proposed overprinted writing, or *écriture portée* [musical notation, polyphony] that sets up a story in breadth rather than length. Thus the text is divided into five voices that each offers their version of the same reality and of the same anxiety: the soul's salvation. As in a musical score, the voices are brought together, woven, sometimes superimposed in harmony or dissonance to take into account, in a way that can be felt, multiple points of view and windows through which we look at the world. This score organizes *linguistic* versions that are distinct from each other not only by what they express (interpretation of an event, reading of what is real), but also by their form (stream of consciousness, dialogue, lists of words without grammatical construction, song, direct address like a talk).

In an undefined place where the dead and the living can coexist, five voices are raised, five bodies come alive. This writing seeks to shed doubt on our perceptions, our interpretations, and our representations of the realm through a sequence that is related to the logic of dreams, of what is dreamt from different windows. The more the show succeeds in shedding light on the multiplicity of points of view, the more it accounts for the extent of non-power we share.

The time of dying becomes eternity; eternity of an imbalance—imbalance of the stance of doubt, eternity of uncertainty in the face of origin as of becoming, eternity of seeking to discover what it's all about.[13] My writing seeks to stage the anarchic reconstitution of the past, and the building of a potential and uncertain future. It turns memory into spectacle.

In taking this text onto the stage, nothing seemed more appropriate to me than to bring it together with Marie Brassard's stage writing. In the course of our conversations, a form gradually emerged in my imagination. I called it *théâtre de l'érosion*. It involves a kind of landscape or relief that transforms almost imperceptibly into a slow and progressive erosion, which leads invariably to denudation [*dénuement*] and to death. (For rocks die too; it's a matter of time.) The denouement of the speech is indeed a denuding or stripping of the words as much as of the images.

What is very stimulating for me is the importance of writings *outside the text* that assume responsibility for a language addressed to all our senses and participation, in the same way as the text, in the construction of this *memory show*.

WHAT COULD BE READ ON STAGE

Joan, a woman about forty years old, is busy at some ordinary task in her apartment. She makes the usual basic gestures. Her actions are those usually taken both in contemporary and bygone circumstances (cleaning up, arranging, sorting, organizing), useful and familiar actions. This is a kind of material theatre. A man

---

13 The author uses here the popular Québec term *rapaillement* associated widely with the poetry of Gaston Miron and his *L'homme rapaillé*. As used by both Miron and de la Chenelière, the word is associated with homely and daily actions taken to tidy up, to stuff the loose straw back into its doll or cushion, or to collect things that have been misplaced, perhaps even lost. It is a particularly powerful metaphor when used to express the reach beyond alienation felt by a person suffering disconnection due to oppressive social values and practices (LHF).

appears and interrupts her; it is Death, who introduces himself to her without forewarning.

At the same time, Joan as a child has a fatal fall from a horse. It is not known which Joan dreams of the other; it is not known which Joan truly dies.

At the same time, Joan's Father speaks of death, which he has already experienced. A ghostly presence, he tries to make his daughter see a bit more clearly.

At the same time, Joan In The Apartment is negotiating with Death to postpone her own demise. She wishes to begin her life again with passion.

At the same time, Joan's Mother is trying to wake her daughter up. A fluttering of eyelids makes her believe that Joan is not dead.

At the same time, Joan In Her Fall imagines she is Joan of Arc with the objective of pleasing her father and of knowing ecstasy.

At the same time, Joan as a child witnesses her father's agony and so decides to not believe in God.

At the same time, during a walk in the forest, Joan's Mother awkwardly teaches the grand principles of existence to her daughter.

At the same time, words fall, like snowflakes, in gentle disorder. I named them *repertories*. It is not known who truly owns these words. They are taken from repertories drawn from the original wall. These are words that recognize no grammar and constitute a kind of radical summary of everything underlying what the show is telling. A strange fluctuating punctuation, this voice embodies the language process of erasure and concealment that is questioning the linguistic edifice and the structures that organize our modes of thinking.

Little by little words grow fewer, the stage empties, night moves in.

JOAN AND JOAN OF ARC

With my reflections forming around the two poles of language and religion, I realized that these elements work simultaneously together in founding and constituting the way I see the world. This is a way of seeing that often makes me feel like a prisoner. By themselves, language and religion sum up the profound discomfort I must live with. And I believe they keep us in the illusion of a common language. Thus, it was natural that *Ravage of Life*, fiction arising from my three years of writing on the wall, pay close attention to these two themes.

I imagined what is deployed in Joan's mind at the moment of her death: a sort of inflation of all the elementary iconography (Catholic and francophone) that forged her imaginary. The show stages a fraction of a second that one guesses to be extremely chaotic, turbulent, violent, Joan plunging into that memory through an injunction that punctuates all her memories: "Look."

Perhaps because my vision is always blurred, eyes were ever-present on the wall, and they are equally so in *Ravage of Life*, perhaps because writing means forcing yourself to look at the world in a sustained way. Writing *is* that fierce and patient gaze on the world. Writing is working at matching that gaze to the point where attention rises above perception. So the gaze is no longer satisfied to gather and report what it sees: it doubts, it contemplates, it breathes, it keeps watch, it tries above all to not be numbed by habit. This gaze requires that we get out of the state of *sideration* where we are kept by the violence of the world. Sideration petrifies us and it authorizes everything since it leaves us without action and without voice. What I seek by writing—and I realize that Joan has the same aspiration—is the road that leads from sideration to desire. It is precisely to kindle desire that Joan will project herself into the passion of Joan of Arc, a passion full of mystery, intensity, contradictions.

The figure of Joan of Arc rapidly imposed itself for its ambiguity, for the political appropriation she has always been used for, for her way of incarnating sanctity, warrior nationalism, torture of martyrs, and thirst for the absolute, which is typical of adolescence, all at the same time, and finally for the erotic charge that her legendary chastity paradoxically provides to her. She represents a coming together of faith and violence, a murky place in which all wars of religion are to be written, all attacks, all assaults committed in the name of chimera humanity invents to exalt itself.

I wanted to make Joan In Her Fall a quintessential adolescent attracted by what could draw her out of an ordinary fate.

TURNAROUND

At the time when I am trying to retrace this journey of creation, I realize that I am turning around, in the manner of my characters, to thinking already enveloped in a thick fog.

I wanted to create a time that was impossible and incessantly torn in its continuity. I wanted to create a place in which recollection is incessantly reconfigured, recollection that memory seeks first to resuscitate, to restore, then to burst apart; a temporality created from thousands of deposits and from as many reversals of an agitated memory.

Often, when you return to writing, you don't manage to pick the train of thought back up. Too impatient, fully engaged in that irrepressible burst, the writer who looks back risks killing thought for fear that it will get away. And yet it is only in this turnaround that hope, the only true engine of writing, can blossom. Hope making thought surge forth from the murky waters into which it has plunged. Hope of restoring life to what has died.

Lot's wife turned around to see Sodom in flames. Orpheus turned back toward Eurydice. The one disobeyed in order to face the disaster, the other to reassure himself that his love was still there. Like her and him, despite all the warnings, I turn around. Stubbornly. Irresistibly.

Disaster and love are powerful lodestones.

Je recomme
sujet verbe c
Exemples de phrases construites avec un sujet, un
les statues
la mer
les mots
qui
qui
qui
qui
qui
qui
recommencent
tombe
tremble
évanouit
échoue
suicide

l'avenir serait-il plus heureux?
une pierre où reposer sa tête.

Ravage of Life

Ravage of Life was first staged in French as *La vie utile* by Espace GO and Festival TransAmériques in collaboration with Infrarouge in Montréal on April 24, 2018. It featured the following cast and creative team:

Christine Beaulieu
Sophie Cadieux
Evelyne de la Chenelière
Louis Negin
Jules Roy-Sicotte

Director: Marie Brassard
Assistant Director: Emmanuelle Kirouac
Set Design: Antonin Sorel
Lighting Design: Sonoyo Nishikawa
Costume Design: UNTTLD (José Manuel St-Jacques + Simon Bélanger)
Makeup and Hair Design: Angelo Barsetti
Music and Sound Design: Jonathan Parant
Sound Processing: Frédéric Auger
Film Production: Karl Lemieux
Film Editing: Guillaume Arseneault
Technical Director: Alex Gendron
Production Director: Line Noël

All of men's misfortune comes from hope, which rips them from the silence of the citadel, which throws them onto the ramparts in the expectation of salvation.

—Albert Camus, *L'homme révolté*

Characters

Joan In The Apartment
Joan In Her Fall
Joan's Mother
Joan's Father
Death

I

The Entrails Of The Earth

JOAN IN THE APARTMENT: I don't know any more when, for the first time, someone told me, or led me to believe, that there is still something else afterward. That after life we don't just become the rotting corpse of ourselves. I felt that someone wanted to give me hope by telling me about a place, a sort of heavenly garden waiting for us, a place of reward and repose that I was shown in paintings and in picture books, the way travel agencies do. I was amazed that you can be both dead and alive somewhere. How can the same body be food for insects and bask in paradise all at the same time? But especially what caused me great anguish was that you absolutely had to believe it in order to make it come true. *If you don't believe it, it won't happen.* That argument seemed untenable to me.

I grew up in a landscape of scarlet and snow and a crown of thorns,[1] and for a long time I expected faith to come. In my imagination it was like a sort of bolt of lightning that hits you and bathes you in a light that never again leaves you. I wanted to be touched by grace, without understanding what that meant exactly. I prayed to God so that He would make me believe in Him.

---

1 Scarlet is the official colour of cardinals' robes in the Catholic Church. According to three of the gospels in the Christian New Testament, a crown of thorns was placed on the head of Jesus at the time of his crucifixion. Joan In The Apartment introduces herself here by evoking the dominant influence of Roman Catholicism in her childhood, thereby positioning herself in the context of the history and traditions of Québec (LHF).

I envied the saints. Especially Saint Francis of Assisi, because he preached to the birds. That means he had faith. In birds. I loved Saint Paul too, because at the beginning of the story he is ugly and mean. And what happened to him led me to believe that I too, contrary to all expectations, could one day become good and charitable like him, that there is hope even for the worst among us, and even for the ugly ones.

Since that bolt of lightning I was calling for wasn't coming, I made believe I had faith. I even managed to do it quite well, I think, but I knew I couldn't fool God Himself. The idea that He might know the truth terrified me. Even so, I plunged into lies with that much more ardour. That's how I turned into a liar. I know it's better to speak truth. But the problem is I can't find words to speak truth, whereas there are lots of words to speak lies.

As soon as I was taught that it takes words to designate the world and all we think of it, communication using language came to seem very complicated to me and quite ambitious. I said to myself that people who claim that they're able to say what they're thinking must not think very much, because language is without the power to convey the boundlessness of living thought, its interruptions, its eternal returns, its incessant convulsions. And maybe common language is the worst of all languages. A common language has always seemed to me to be, in spite of what it claims, the place of incomprehension among people, and the source of all misunderstandings. In other words, speaking the same language is all it takes for mutual incomprehension. In fact, I have always found that language gives a final and irrevocable character to reality. Language is without the power to adapt to the world as I perceive it: turbid, uncertain, changing.

All that, as a child I couldn't say it, and yet I really believe I thought it. Ever since I've been wondering: So what was that language I was thinking in before I began to speak? That's maybe where I would like to begin again from. From that language I know nothing about, that language from before the mother tongue that wound up filling all the room in my head. I would like to begin everything again because I'm dreaming of a new past much more than a lovely future.

Before what do I need to come back to
Before what beginning
To what do I need set fire so as to be reborn from my ashes

I begin again.

In the beginning, no Word, but a scent of dead leaves—without the death of even a single leaf . . . since there would not yet be leaves, since we are at the beginning. A fragrance of dead leaves, without dead leaves. A fragrance boding decomposition to warn that the beginning is already an end. The first day a fragrance of flies and dead leaves was emanating on its principle. The wind carried the fragrance and shook it in a swirl whose continuous movement created a sweet-smelling and warm ball. From the belly of the Earth creatures emerged destined to be food for the leaves: lions, frogs, oysters, horses, and us as well, snakes, monkeys, wolves, cicadas, and all that breathed the heady fragrance of the dead leaves. Soon, sounds joined the fragrance. Quiverings, breaths, songs, laughs, groans, rattles, beats, bangings, cadences, all that soared into infinity. And all the creatures were living in the sound of their own movements, and in the fragrance of death, so that they would always remember they were meant to be food for the leaves and the flies. The creatures took pity on themselves, pity for making so much noise for nothing. They prayed to no longer know about their own death, despite its heady fragrance, to forget that, when their time came to an end, they would be eaten by the leaves and the flies. Their prayer was granted. Since then, we are born to die, we live in the illusion of our eternity.

I begin again.

Everything would be different if we lived inside our skeleton rather than outside it; everything would be different if we were made like shellfish and crustaceans. Skeleton outside. We would see our death . . .

The rest of JOAN IN THE APARTMENT*'s words are muffled in some way by* JOAN'S FATHER*'s.*

. . . imminent every day, in every mirror; we would have time to get used to the idea; we would cease hoping for the salvation of our soul. The problem is that we are put together wrong side out; we are pieces put together that would be beautiful seen overturned, so as to show our bones while sowing a bit of meat as they pass; it would be a fantastic upset. We would wear our skeleton like an ornament, like a trophy, like striking proof of our eternity. And then humanity on the march would be a parade of bones, a procession of fossils. We would take our skeleton out for a walk. It would give a full toothy smile as though telling us that in the end there is nothing to fear, nor to hope for.

JOAN'S FATHER: And suddenly, you fall. You fall into a fault in the earth. The jaw of the place squeezes in on you. You feel the breath of your fall. You slide into the throat of the Earth. At the end of your fall, there is yet another fall, and so on, as in a dream of falling, as when you dream you are falling endlessly. But this time something interrupts your fall, immobilizes you. There you are in the entrails of the Earth. You look. You wonder whether everything is there. After all, where do the dead go? What belly is large enough to hold them all? Where do their eyes go? Where do the mouths that devoured them go? And you keep on falling. You begin again to fall without end. There you are in the eternity of your fall.

JOAN'S MOTHER: Joan
Joan
She opened her eyes I'm not dreaming
Joan
Joan I'm your mother
Here is your bedroom

JOAN IN THE APARTMENT: My father makes mysterious statements.

JOAN'S FATHER: You must watch out for the tricks that desire plays on morality.

JOAN IN THE APARTMENT: He always falls in love with magnificent men
Much younger than he is
And in order to be successful in loving the voluptuous and nude body of my mother
That he must penetrate whatever the cost
So that I come into being
So that something is drawn from her entrails
He closes his eyes in the same way you clench your teeth

JOAN IN HER FALL: I emerge from my mother's entrails
I feel immediately that something is wrong

I look at the world and the course of its history seems impossible
  for me to catch up with
Useless effort
I'm dumbfounded and I don't know what to respond
I'm afraid of sinking into the future
I choose to take refuge in indifference and moderation
I work out kinds of limbos for myself that protect me both from
  suffering and from rapture
And I make the firm decision to be without fear and without hope
As a child I am ugly
But my mother shows me off
She brandishes me like proof

JOAN'S MOTHER: Look
Her name is Joan she's my daughter
Her name is Joan like Joan of Arc
She is certainly her father's daughter

JOAN IN HER FALL: I am proof that my mother by dint of contortions
Was able to give my father a taste for her entrails
My father seldom looks at me
He dedicates a cult to Saint Joan of Arc
Perhaps because she is like a boy
There are hangings on the walls of the apartment
All kinds of images of Joan of Arc
On horseback
On foot
At the stake
Armed with a sword
On her knees
In prison
In rapture

My father often tells me
The story of her extraordinary fate as a warrior
And her prodigious ride
Joan of Arc is
An adolescent like me
A runaway who drove her parents mad
I don't have her courage and I envy her
I am envious and I envy her
For her passion
For her faith
For her superhuman drive
For her heroic violence and her peasantry
And I hate her for pleasing my father so powerfully instead of pleasing her own
Among all her exploits
It's her virginity that impresses me the most
What willpower
I who am in such a rush
Such a rush to commit the sin of lust
That's all I think about
When I see my father's handsome lovers file past

JOAN'S MOTHER: Close your mouth when you're not speaking, Joan. Keeping your mouth open like that makes you look like a moron.

DEATH sings.

JOAN IN THE APARTMENT: Are you an apparition? I've been hoping for an apparition for so long . . . I have always dreamt of hearing voices that tell me how to act and where to go, that guide me and guarantee me a road toward what is fair and good. I would have obeyed them; I'm going to obey you, you'll see. Anyway, freedom makes me anxious. What can be done with free will, and in what direction can steps be taken, when it's known that sin is everywhere, that existence is a minefield and that even so we have to keep moving forward in the dark? It's dark, isn't it?

DEATH: You have to come with me, Joan.[2]

JOAN IN THE APARTMENT: And it's now?

DEATH: Yes.

JOAN IN THE APARTMENT: I should have expected as much. I was born with a bad premonition. Which everything then confirmed. May I at least take your coat? Do you have a minute? You're not keeping track down to the smallest minute? It's really dark here.

JOAN'S MOTHER: Joan
Joan
She opened her eyes I'm not dreaming
Joan
Joan I'm your mother
Here is your bedroom
And your horse is dead
You must stay in your room now
Patience
Look
That's a window over there
You see

2 Death speaks English throughout the French version. Other than changing the character's name from Jeanne to Joan in this translation, I have made only minimal changes from the original in Death's lines (LHF).

A window looks like a breach in a wall
With a window
You can open the window
Let the wind come in
You can close it too
You can make day and make night
By opening or closing the shutters
With a window
You can look outside
Or look at yourself
The reflection of yourself
In the window's pane
With a window
You can look at the drops sliding
Down the window
When it rains
Then you can place a bet on a drop
Like on a racehorse
And win
With a window
You can wash the window
So you can see better
With a window
You can throw yourself out of the window
In despair
On a bad day
With a window
You can wave goodbye with your hand
To someone who is leaving
Who is passing by
Who is arriving
With a window

You can imagine that the window
Looks out on the sea
With a window
You can see the death of a bird
Who banged into the window
Since a window looks like a breach in a wall
And deceives the birds

JOAN IN THE APARTMENT: Excuse me, things are in such a mess here.

JOAN IN THE APARTMENT busies herself making gestures that are not necessarily comprehensible.

Everything always needs a new beginning, have you noticed? I really like doing usual things. Material life reassures me because it is perishable. It offers a sort of guarantee. It gives the impression of making a difference. Do you find me superficial?

DEATH: No.

JOAN IN THE APARTMENT: And yet I am. I believe that I am.

JOAN IN THE APARTMENT stops what she is doing all of a sudden.

To be frank, you are disturbing me. I hate surprises and I wasn't expecting you.

DEATH: I am rarely expected.

JOAN IN THE APARTMENT: *(for herself, looking around)* My God, everything moves.

DEATH: Sometimes I am being called.

JOAN IN THE APARTMENT: Pardon?

DEATH: Sometimes, people call me.

JOAN IN THE APARTMENT: Not me. I did not call you.

DEATH: Do you believe in God?

JOAN IN THE APARTMENT: Should I?

JOAN'S FATHER: A horseback ride. You fall off the horse. You bang your head on a large stone. You fall into a fold of time. You have a very long sleep. You open your eyes for a fraction of a second. The day blinds you immediately, but your mother insists. She says "look, look" to you, and she points her finger at where you're supposed to look. You keep on falling.

JOAN'S MOTHER: Look at the flower, look at the cat, look at the bird. Don't look at the sun, it's dangerous. Look at the ocean; it's where the world began. Look, look at this reflection; it's you.

JOAN'S FATHER: Your mother is teaching you what is beautiful.

JOAN'S MOTHER: Look at this beautiful flower; look at this pretty little cat; look at this lovely bird. No, you don't say « le beau oiseau », you say « le bel oiseau », it's a question of euphony. Look at the sea, it's big and it's endless, it's eternal, so it's beautiful, touch it, you can touch it, it's water, it's wet, it sparkles, it's foam, that you can touch, it's cold, it's snow, it's soft, no don't touch that, it's dirty, don't touch it, it's fragile, don't touch your food, you must eat it, you don't play with your food; you eat it, eat your vegetables, eat your meat, it's horse meat, it's good for your health. Later, you must sleep, close your eyes, sleep now, you must sleep; we'll pick this all up again tomorrow.

JOAN IN HER FALL: I look out the window that looks like a breach in a wall
I look at the people walking by
People are always carrying dragging pushing or pulling something
A bag
A suitcase
A leash
A child
A pitcher
A lamp
A slave
A gun
And then I have difficulty recognizing the shape of people
I see only illegible shadows
Clusters and extensions
Indecipherable
People don't look like my mother's drawings

JOAN'S MOTHER: Look, Joan.

JOAN IN HER FALL: My mother teaches me the shape of people
She draws a round head and straight legs

JOAN'S MOTHER: *(reading a book to JOAN)* Paul is a boy. Paul est un garçon.

JOAN IN HER FALL: Next, she draws hair and a skirt

JOAN'S MOTHER: Joan is a girl. Jeanne est une fille.

JOAN IN HER FALL: My mother reads me stories.

JOAN'S MOTHER: *(still reading the same book)* Heaven is blue and filled with angels
The earth is dirty and full of enemies
Early in the morning
The goat is devoured by the wolf
The lovers took poison
Everyone is dead and no one has learned anything
Good night

JOAN IN HER FALL: I would rather look out the window

JOAN'S FATHER: If we traced lines that have connected human footsteps
Since the beginning of time
Since we have been walking upright
Since we have been walking and incessantly retracing our steps
Without knowing it
Like people lost in a forest eyes filled with fright
Since we have been walking
On sand
On snow
On dust
On sidewalks
The North pillaging the South
The South running aground in the North

Exiles conquests meanders and crusades
If we traced lines to connect all those footsteps
A design would jump out telling
What we have always been looking for
This design made of lines so numerous and entangled
Would show a gigantic stain
A shadow
The black flower of what we have been seeking for millennia

JOAN IN HER FALL: Seeking for wood
Seeking for water
Seeking for wood
Seeking for water
Seeking for wood
Seeking for water
Seeking for wood
Seeking for water
Seeking for salt
Seeking for gold
Seeking for milk
Seeking for wheat
Seeking for berries
Seeking for eggs
Seeking for wild game
Seeking for burrows
Seeking for fish
Flow
Wind
Light
Fire
Spices
The deer

The antelope
The coyote
The wolf
The animal
The barbarian
The savage
The Indian
The monster
The enemy
The assassin
The infidel
The heretic
The non-believer
The dissenter
The invader
The scoundrel
Evil
The bad guy

DEATH: You said, "My God."

JOAN IN THE APARTMENT: When?

DEATH: "My God, everything moves."

JOAN IN THE APARTMENT moves toward the window, which looks like a breach in a wall.

JOAN IN THE APARTMENT: That's nothing. That doesn't mean anything: "My God," it's a sort of punctuation. It keeps things going. When you're speaking. Can I offer you something to drink?

DEATH: With pleasure.

JOAN IN THE APARTMENT: And you? Do you believe in God?

DEATH: It makes it possible to acknowledge the rest.

JOAN IN THE APARTMENT: I'm not so sure about that.

JOAN IN THE APARTMENT looks out the window.

That's the way you see us?

DEATH: How?

JOAN IN THE APARTMENT: You look at us from a sort of window, sheltered from the storm? You observe us like insects blinded by the light of day? Is that the way you see us? Do you lay a bet on one of us? Who is winning the race?

DEATH: Hard to say.

JOAN IN THE APARTMENT: You watch us not knowing how to live? That's it? You watch us struggling and carrying our bad conscience everywhere with us? Does that amuse you? Are you sorry about that? Does that upset you? Does that make you feel pity? Scorn? What do we make you feel? Do we touch you? That's it, we touch you? It's been a long time since I was touched. I would really like that. To be touched. By others. I mean: touched by the fate of others. I would really like to see what can be seen from your window. As for me, where I look from, what I see means nothing to me. Other people mean nothing to me.

JOAN'S FATHER: But what we're looking for
Much more than water
Wood wheat and the scoundrel
Is the salvation of our soul
For always and ever since always
The salvation of our soul
Project for a whole useful life
The only genuine project
Source of our symptoms and our monuments
A whole life to prepare its fate
Carve tombstones taking you straight to heaven
Set eternal and precious stones in them
Draw wings that make the legs longer
And what do you need to take with you?
Offer wine and gold to the gods
A son a lamb
Beseech give thanks and believe
Believe and fear
Believe and fear
Fear and hope
Hope and believe
Believe and keep on believing
Because we cannot resign ourselves to becoming nothing more than a corpse
It would be too horrible
And the idea of our flesh melting on its skeleton
Is unbearable to us
We must believe and walk
And we walk
While we wonder where to direct our steps
And we follow each other one after the other

The blind leading the blind
All we know is to follow
In the walking and the stopping
We follow each other
Making the same stops before the same abyss
We all seem to know precisely what we are doing
Where we are walking to
We have a pace
A direction
If we spot a hesitant gait
We take a detour
So as to not follow those steps
Especially to not follow the steps of those who limp
Especially to know how to turn away in time
From the path of madness
And sometimes something
Perhaps vertigo
Pushes us into each others' arms
We embrace a body in order to make it necessary
It seems that then we love

JOAN IN HER FALL: I'm not sure about that.

JOAN'S MOTHER: Joan?

JOAN IN HER FALL: Men in grey suits
Whisper and smoke around the bed
They are my father's lovers
They are younger than my mother
They are handsome
My mother serves them coffee

JOAN'S MOTHER: I have forgiven everything.

JOAN IN THE APARTMENT: My father has his eyes closed and his mouth open
He's in a rush to suffer since he has almost no time left to win his heaven

JOAN'S MOTHER: I forgive you, my darling.

JOAN IN HER FALL: I look at my father and I wonder whether he will have a right to paradise
I wonder whether God will punish my father for his love of men

JOAN'S MOTHER: Give your father something to drink, Joan.

JOAN IN THE APARTMENT: I pick up the sponge on a stick soaked with water
My father's lovers watch me

JOAN'S MOTHER: Give him something to drink.

JOAN IN HER FALL: Over the bed
A picture of Joan of Arc
She frightens me and I wonder what my father sees in her
I look at my father
The cancer has already eaten his muscles his fat and the inside of all his bones

JOAN'S MOTHER: I have forgiven everything.

JOAN IN HER FALL: My mother seems to take great pride in the non-stop forgiveness she grants to everyone.

JOAN'S MOTHER: You can depart in peace.

JOAN IN THE APARTMENT: I look at my mother and I can't help but think of her nude and voluptuous body.

JOAN'S MOTHER: What do you want from me, Joan? Close your mouth a bit when you're looking at me.

JOAN IN HER FALL: To think that my father had to penetrate that body so that I would happen
To think that my father penetrated my mother's body to draw something from her entrails

JOAN'S MOTHER: Give your father something to drink.

JOAN IN HER FALL: My father is turning himself into a martyr
He is allowing himself to be devoured
By the cancer
Without treatment and without morphine
Believing that only suffering
Will cleanse his soul from all his sins of lust
And will give him a right to heaven
Nothing will remain of him
But a widow ashamed
Of having been the wife of my father

JOAN'S MOTHER: *(with false humility)* I have forgiven everything.

JOAN IN HER FALL: My father is skinny
He resembles a sketch
He doesn't talk anymore
I can no longer take him at his word

JOAN'S MOTHER: Give your father something to drink, Joan.

JOAN IN HER FALL: I pick up the sponge on a stick soaked with water
My father's lips are brown and chapped
I move toward the mouth until it is no longer a mouth
It is a drought
It is a landscapc
It is cracked soil with crusts of black silt in spots
I flood the desert
Water fills the cracks
Then overflows
The gullies start to vomit out muddy torrents
My father chokes
I hear the sound of his voice
It is finally speaking truth
All it says is that the water went down the wrong way and that my father does not want to die

JOAN'S MOTHER: Hey, stop, you're going to drown him! Don't drown your father! Stop!

2

Ruins Yet To Come

JOAN IN HER FALL: Ruins of forest
Ruins of trees
Ruins of roots
Ruins of Laurentian flora
Ruins of natural history
Ruins of ravage[3]
Ruins of deer
Ruins of birds
Ruins of hares
Ruins of mushrooms
Ruins of dead leaves
Ruins of green leaves
Ruins of stream
Ruins of moss
Ruins of stone
Ruins of forest garlic
Ruins of buttercups
Ruins of horses
Ruins of hair
Ruins of eyes
Ruins of teeth
Ruins of gowns
Ruins of my mother
Ruins of ruins

---

3 In Québec and elsewhere in francophone Canada, one meaning of the word *ravage* is "aire d'hivernage de certains animaux auvages" [hibernation site of some wild animals such as deer or antelope], a meaning that has particular resonance in *Ravage of Life* (LHF).

JOAN'S MOTHER: Look Joan
Those are paths
Since we must be sure to tame what grows
Otherwise the forest will grow black and impenetrable
Don't step off the path
There is always a forest waiting to harm us
It is taking its revenge for all the earth
We have stolen from it
If you are silent
You might see a wild animal
Maybe even a deer
But the deer hides
It distrusts
It has known from the first day
That man is a predator
That you and I my darling
We have carried the smell of blood for millennia
Yes
Even you
You have already eaten ham haven't you
Well there's little chance that you'll see a deer
But you can look at the plants and the flowers
Who don't run away
Poor flowers
Poor things they don't know how to run away
Look

JOAN IN HER FALL: My mother takes me for a walk in the forest
She says to me
Look

JOAN'S MOTHER: Look.

JOAN IN HER FALL: And everywhere that I cast my eyes
I see only ruins

JOAN'S MOTHER: Look how beautiful it is, look!

JOAN IN HER FALL: My mother teaches me flowers. She tells me that the fir is an evergreen tree. She tells me that Indigenous people call the *Achillea millefolium* "squirrel's tail."

JOAN'S MOTHER: Look at its fluffy little curved leaves; it's true that you'd say little squirrels' tails, don't you think so?

JOAN IN HER FALL: I don't think so. My mother tells me that the female orange-coloured sparrowhawk has fluff to protect her from the cold, and that you are not supposed to pick forest garlic.

JOAN'S MOTHER: Forest garlic has become a vulnerable species because of the excessive appetite of humans. They take too much of everything.

JOAN IN HER FALL: My mother holds my hand and I do the same for her, even if we don't know how to do it.

JOAN'S MOTHER: Oh, look, Joan!

JOAN IN HER FALL: My mother shows me a white flower.

JOAN'S MOTHER: Do you see that flower? The French call it *le sabot de la Vierge.*[4]

JOAN IN HER FALL: The flower is watching me.

JOAN'S MOTHER: Le sabot de la Vierge. Do you see? God is everywhere, even in the forest.

JOAN IN HER FALL: God is watching me.

JOAN'S MOTHER: God is everywhere and sees everything, even in your head. Nothing escapes Him, not even the dreams you have; you can sleep peacefully. You are never alone, never, never. Even in your grave, the eye of God will be there. Close your mouth when you're not speaking, Joan. Keeping your mouth open like that makes you look like a moron.

JOAN IN HER FALL: When my mother isn't looking anymore, I crush le sabot de la Vierge. But God saw me.

JOAN'S MOTHER: What is it, Joan?

JOAN IN HER FALL: I keep my mouth open in stunned amazement and I stare at my mother.

JOAN'S MOTHER: What is it, Joan?

JOAN IN HER FALL: I don't take my eyes off her.

---

4 *Le sabot de la Vierge* ("the Virgin's slipper") is called "lady's slipper" in English (LHF).

JOAN'S MOTHER: What is it?

JOAN IN HER FALL: She's speaking to me. Pardon?

JOAN'S MOTHER: What is it?

JOAN IN HER FALL: What?

JOAN'S MOTHER: What is it?

JOAN IN HER FALL: What?

JOAN'S MOTHER: What is it?

JOAN IN HER FALL: What is what?!

JOAN'S MOTHER: What is it?!

JOAN IN HER FALL: I don't understand anything she's saying.

JOAN'S MOTHER: No no we are not lost
Stop crying
I'm telling you that we are not lost

JOAN IN THE APARTMENT: The eye was in the tomb and stared at Cain. This is terrible, this eye that follows you all the way to the tomb, all the way into your nights, all the way into your darkest thoughts, all the way into your basest, most shameful desires . . . don't you think so?

She speaks to DEATH.

You're not very talkative. Truth be told, though, you're right.

They drink, then JOAN cannot help herself from breaking the silence.

In my imagination, I didn't see you like this. I imagined you more impressive.

DEATH: No need.

JOAN IN THE APARTMENT: Your name is enough.

DEATH: I don't have a name.

JOAN IN THE APARTMENT: You have no name? What luck. I would like . . . to not have a name. Can you imagine all the potential of a thing that has no name? Names deceive you. Just like teeth. When someone sends a smile my way, I think that person wants to bite me. And the other way around. Hard to tell. I often have this dream where all my teeth come detached and fall to the ground. Teeth rain from my mouth; too many teeth for one mouth. My mother appears, she looks at the ground strewn with teeth, and says, "Isn't that a beautiful smile?" Then she looks at me and asks me: "What is your name?" And then I choose my name to answer her. I choose a toothless name like me; I answer my mother that my name is Palm, that I am totally Palm and that everyone calls me Palm. I am a thing that can only open and bleed. I was born with wrinkles, three deep lines where the future can be read. I am offering and softness. My mother tells me that Palm is no name for a girl before she gathers up my teeth and leaves.

JOAN'S FATHER: Maybe your horse suddenly realized the extent of his enslavement and felt the weight of his load. Maybe a flash of lucidity. Maybe a sharp pain. Maybe an ancestral burden. We just don't know. We cannot know, we are not horses. It seems that horses remember.

JOAN'S MOTHER: Don't cry
My darling
No the horse does not suffer under your weight
A horse likes to be led
God told us to submit animals to our desires and to our appetite
God created the animals
And then He created us so that we would give a name to the animals
So that we would give them a name and that they belong to us
Their flesh is ours
Their fur
Their force
Their oil
Their skin
Their teeth
Their milk
Their eggs
Their honey
We are to be served
Serve yourself
My darling
Serve yourself well
In the end it will be them
The animals
Who will empty your icy and sticky corpse
They will roll you over and empty you like a pouch
Until then serve yourself well

JOAN'S FATHER: You were born into a world where everything already had a name: the slightest shape, the slightest colour. You have hardly been born when you are informed that everything has a name.

JOAN IN HER FALL: I'm disappointed.

JOAN'S MOTHER: There are all kinds of things, and all things have a name. Things belonging to the past are called relics. Things belonging to someone are called coveted objects; things that don't belong to anyone anymore are called lost items; things belonging to everyone are called the common good; things that you receive from a dead person are called heritage. You see, things can be a thousand things, and all things have in common their impermanence. You as well. You as well, you're going to die. Of course, of course, patience.

JOAN'S FATHER: And you're taught the names.

JOAN IN HER FALL: There are many names.

JOAN'S FATHER: And you're taught the genders.

JOAN IN HER FALL: There are two genders.

JOAN'S FATHER: And you're taught that in French that some nouns are feminine and some are masculine.

JOAN IN HER FALL: I'm told that the moon is feminine while the sun is masculine.

JOAN'S MOTHER: The moon is pale and the sun shines.

JOAN IN HER FALL: I try to not draw conclusions.

JOAN'S MOTHER: Some words are invariable: they last, they are stable, they don't get upset, either in front of or after a feminine word; they don't allow themselves to be impressed by a plural, they don't spend their lives adapting themselves to others.

JOAN IN HER FALL: They are inflexible and unshakable.

JOAN'S MOTHER: They are steady and reliable.

JOAN IN HER FALL: They are radical and self-satisfied.

JOAN'S MOTHER: Always.

JOAN IN HER FALL: Never.

JOAN'S MOTHER: Perhaps.

JOAN IN HER FALL: Too late.

JOAN'S FATHER: You learn you can't choose a name for things
You can't name what's around you as you like
Nor people you meet
You were thinking that by naming things you could make their reality more flexible

JOAN IN HER FALL: Things are merciless
You can't choose anything

JOAN'S MOTHER: We looked for your name for a long time

JOAN IN HER FALL: I would at least like to be able to choose my own name.

JOAN'S MOTHER: A name that uplifts you.

JOAN IN HER FALL: A name that dooms me.

JOAN'S MOTHER: Blanche, Grace, Mary.

JOAN IN HER FALL: Phaedra, Medea, Ophelia.

JOAN'S MOTHER: But we chose Joan to make your father happy . . . whom I have completely forgiven.

JOAN IN HER FALL: I would like to be Joan of Arc's horse
I would like to be the horse that carries me
He is agile and has no name
His tail is the train of an elegant dress
His mane is made of mingled streams
His teeth are white seashells
And his coat a dark cloud
This is not one horse
It is ten horses
One hundred horses
It is a herd
Without contour and without name

JOAN'S MOTHER: Joan
Joan
She opened her eyes I'm not dreaming

JOAN'S FATHER: Warhorses and workhorses
Horses of the Indians of America
Horses of the Arabs of the desert
Horses of the Zouaves and squads
Circus horses with feathers and sequins
Hunting horses and packs of dogs
Carriage horses for princes for executioners to draw and quarter
Centaurs and seahorses
Winged horses touching the sun
Racehorses spitting foam
Mad horses hit by the spear bitten by the serpent
Horses like stains in our winters in painting
Horses straddled by faith
Horses petrified in bronze and marble
October horses sacrificed on the Champ de Mars
Their head sliced then crowned with bread
Horses cut into quarters of red and ferrous meat
Horses for quartering of torture victims
Horses that have their eyes put out so we can believe in them

JOAN IN HER FALL: I never take off my armour
I grow thin in it
My horse is grateful for my lightness
He gallops while following the holy voices
That tell me where to go
And whom to fight
My parents are furious and distraught
They curse my adolescence

They understand nothing
But they'll see what I'm capable of
I'll be rewarded
I'll free my country of invaders
I'll be celebrated after my death
For having made the blood of the enemy flow
And also for never having made my own flow
My own blood will never flow
I shall never be like my mother
Producing fruit in my entrails destined to rot
That was always repugnant to me to be the fruit of my mother's womb
I am disgusted by my blood
Horrified at being a network of bowels
I am terrified by my own teeth
I try to forget they exist by drinking nothing but broth
I am afraid of my skeleton that keeps itself inside me and watches me
There are those who want to make me eat
Want to see me grow
Want my body to become capable of producing eggs
And milk eventually
And want in turn for my womb to bear fruit it's enough to make you vomit

JOAN'S MOTHER: What are you thinking about, my darling?

JOAN IN HER FALL: I would really have liked you to abort

JOAN'S MOTHER: Oh yes you like to take a walk in the forest with Mommy
It's beautiful isn't it

JOAN IN HER FALL: Then I would have died without ever having been born
Before this inconceivable catastrophe of separation
That makes us shout out our distress and incredulity
From the first to the last day
In limbo the aborted are at peace
They don't know how to feel either fear or hope
I like the shyness of the bones and the teeth in aborted babies
I like that their face is at first just eyelids and lips
I like especially that they do not speak
I would be silent like them
They are not encumbered by words nor by their teeth
Their teeth are like buds that will never bloom
Little bulbs that would become knives
If the mouth came into bloom
Burgeoning knives between the lips
Teeth make us bite or smile depending on the occasion
Besides we would each need two mouths
One for smiling and the other for biting
There would be less confusion

JOAN'S MOTHER: Close your mouth when you're not speaking, Joan, you look like a moron keeping your mouth open like that.

JOAN IN HER FALL: My mother is beautiful in her skin and her hair.

JOAN'S MOTHER: Thank you, my darling.

JOAN IN HER FALL: But underneath, inside, in my mother, there are terrifying things; I know, I was there.

JOAN'S MOTHER: And that's how babies are made.

JOAN IN HER FALL: You guys too?!

JOAN'S MOTHER: Obviously, us too, Joan! What do you think?

JOAN IN HER FALL: I can't believe it, it's unbelievable.

JOAN'S MOTHER: I know, it's disgusting, but that's the way it is.

JOAN'S FATHER: Remember Joan
God created by separating the elements
Fusion horrifies Him
Peace will come to pass in the separation of things
In any case two species who have nothing in common are not put
Into the same cage
A wolf and a wild boar are not obliged
To live together
Don't let yourself be moved by the first one who comes the first innocent the first one who drowned
Shoo him away Joan
Shoo him away or he will eat you

JOAN'S MOTHER: Beware Joan
Of intrusions
Don't go wallowing in another's flesh
And keep yourself impenetrable
We are made of so many orifices
So many openings that dilate with the slightest excitement
A breach is always an excess
Don't let someone else flow and spread himself in you

Otherwise soon you won't know anymore what you're made of
Tear access to your sacred flesh
To your clear and pure blood from men
One day a man will say to you
Don't be afraid there's nothing to be afraid of just relax
It's only a distaff a reed a cotton spindle
But in truth believe me it's a stake it's a horn it's a snake
Beware
Believe me and beware

JOAN IN HER FALL: Nothing touches me
Neither grace nor anyone
So I decide that I will be chaste
Pure enough to cut my fingers off
I'm bored
I invent apparitions that command me to act
And to purify the world
With weapons if need be
I am an adolescent
Banality horrifies me
My scream is waiting to find its voice
The world cannot be named yet I wish to speak it

JOAN'S MOTHER: Close your mouth, my darling. Close your mouth when you're not speaking, otherwise you'll be swallowing flies; that's all they're waiting for.

3

The Equations

JOAN IN THE APARTMENT: I don't want to. I don't agree.

DEATH: It's not about agreeing.

JOAN IN THE APARTMENT: Can we find something else?

DEATH: It's amazing how people never want to die.

JOAN IN THE APARTMENT: I would like . . .

DEATH: *(interrupting her)* And want to heal from everything.

JOAN IN THE APARTMENT: Is it . . .

DEATH: *(interrupting again)* While living is an incurable disease.

JOAN IN THE APARTMENT: Yes, but it's because I haven't finished . . .

DEATH: *(interrupting her once more)* We all die before we are done with something. We die and, inevitably, something else is not finished.

JOAN IN THE APARTMENT: Even so, I could die a bit later.

DEATH: I don't want to be brutal, but what do you have to do? What did you not finish?

JOAN IN THE APARTMENT: The round. The revolution.

DEATH: You?

JOAN IN THE APARTMENT: I'm talking about a discrete revolution, like the one stars and planets make.

DEATH: Everything dies. Even revolutions.

JOAN IN THE APARTMENT: Okay, but can I have the time?

DEATH: How much?

JOAN IN THE APARTMENT: What?

DEATH: How long?

JOAN IN HER FALL: I don't sleep I never sleep
I don't close my eyes
Not a single blink
I cut out two eyelids
In tissue paper
That I place on my eyes
To make the world and my parents believe
That I am sleeping
While I am looking

JOAN'S MOTHER: Look, Joan.

JOAN IN HER FALL: My eyes are wide open
On the obscenity of the world
On the nature of things
And their useful life

JOAN'S MOTHER: Look: this part of the forest has been burned.

JOAN IN HER FALL: I hate everything I look at
Everything that penetrates my eyes burns me

JOAN'S MOTHER: Man sets fire to the forest to prepare the soil for culture.

JOAN IN HER FALL: I detest this nature that we imitate

JOAN'S MOTHER: The ashes feed the earth so that it can feed us in turn.

JOAN IN HER FALL: All we are doing is copying the dark side of nature

JOAN'S MOTHER: Do you see?

JOAN IN HER FALL: All we are doing is reproducing the cruel side of things

JOAN'S MOTHER: We are full of ingenuity when it comes to not dying.

JOAN IN HER FALL: A constant succession where everybody eats everybody

JOAN'S MOTHER: Can you see the little shoots? They are morels. They were born from a fire. Nature is an unfathomable mystery.

JOAN IN HER FALL: I would like to disrupt its plans
Disobey its laws
Destroy its reign

JOAN'S MOTHER: Isn't it beautiful?

JOAN IN HER FALL: Through my gaze I'll succeed in dissolving the nature of things
To the point of life transforming itself into a dream

JOAN'S MOTHER: Joan
Joan
She has opened her eyes I'm not dreaming
Joan

JOAN IN HER FALL: a b c d e f g h i j k l m n o p q r s t u v w x y z insufficient begin again come back repent print failure again knead flesh verb scarlet snow crown thorn stir take back beginning grammar writing sound shout subject word complement regret past remorse time sew failure lie speak future course choose teaching meal disappear stupour truth contemplate guarantee born again ashes fire maid wise devoted lack sky earth believe understand statue sea word name water leaf horizon people God distressed cloud work catastrophe dread fullness rib reed wizard apprentice morale story pride desire power disobedience master slave flash goat princess mermaid good night sweet dreams origin speech dismemberment punishment pity new beginning zero one two three four five six seven shadows abyss clay earth light day night evening morning sky firmament separation of the waters sea continent tree star season fish sea monster bird pets reptile snake man woman sin regret patience unfinishable tentative senseless restore world wall vacation humiliation partition gulf inscription grotto gravedigger bone bird fish catechesis eternity perpetuity always vice odious immortal concupiscence grace faith belief proof vision assault demon courage debris eye tomb possess destroy depose rob deprive reign kill benevolence mercy genesis scent augur illusion bear frog oyster horse monkey wolf cicada creature trembling breath song laughter groan beat slamming fall infinity sound egg fly lack love sin prayer die lack throat sin ruthless cartography turn back upset time ghost fault thing consistency too little too late maybe because already always bird trace repent French Hebrew Arabic cross-eyed swelling tongue tooth jaw dream threat miracle invariable fault constancy endurance haste astonishment apocalypse prophesy revelation final judgment bad day reed morale obscenity hope light fertile flourishing longing gluttony predation weakness nasty eat blood silver gold usage time tongue flesh throne moon dragon crown clothes harp star candle holder angel door slit throat lamb white rust greenish horn sun king gap wall speak tirelessly recreate everything more more more more still more

DEATH: So: How long? How much more do you want? You don't know what to answer, you don't know how to say how much, you only know how to say more. And who to die in your place?

JOAN IN THE APARTMENT: To die in my place?

DEATH: Yes.

JOAN IN THE APARTMENT: No one!

DEATH: But you have to.

JOAN IN THE APARTMENT: Why?

DEATH: Balance issue.

JOAN IN THE APARTMENT: Thinking like an accountant.

DEATH: There are only equations.

JOAN IN THE APARTMENT: I'm not going to condemn someone just to please you.

DEATH: Are you afraid of hell?

JOAN IN THE APARTMENT: No more than of paradise. I dislike extremes.

DEATH: Oh, good.

JOAN IN THE APARTMENT: I want to go to limbo.

DEATH: Why?

JOAN IN THE APARTMENT: I like what is vague.

DEATH: You like the haze.

JOAN IN THE APARTMENT: Yes. Limbo, not much is known, it's uncertain, you wander, you float; it's not ecstasy, but then again neither is it suffering.

DEATH: You are a woman of compromises.

JOAN IN THE APARTMENT: I would have liked to be radical, but I can't do it. I'm undecided.

DEATH: There is no more limbo.

JOAN IN THE APARTMENT: What?

DEATH: It doesn't exist anymore.

JOAN IN THE APARTMENT: There is no more limbo?

DEATH: The Vatican decided that it no longer exists.

JOAN IN THE APARTMENT: Why?

DEATH: So that the dead children without baptism can go straight to paradise.

JOAN IN THE APARTMENT: But they were doing just fine in limbo!

DEATH: You think so?

JOAN IN THE APARTMENT: They were calm. They knew nothing of hope.

DEATH: You don't want to hope?

JOAN IN THE APARTMENT: No, because as soon as you hope, you fear. You fear that something will happen or will not happen. I like the idea of limbo precisely because of the absence of hope.

I can see myself floating there with tiny children, some of them the size of shrimp, all together in permanent indetermination, in an infinitely prolonged interval, for centuries of centuries, swimming in a milk that I imagine almost white, neither saved nor damned, without flames and without bliss. Since I have the same dread for both, flames for obvious reasons, bliss because the image I make of it is grotesque and vaguely erotic. That makes me uncomfortable. Ecstasy and bliss keep your mouth open, while it's a thing I'm trying to correct; I speak with my mouth open, fixing a stupefied look on my face. The thing is that the world surprises me so much that I can't get over it. I can't get over anything. But I'm no longer startled, I don't get indignant anymore—contrary to what should happen. The world is a scandal and I don't know how to be scandalized; history is a succession of outrages. But even though I call with my whole soul for that state of indignation, the state that seems to be the only good response to the spectacle offered to us, I remain blocked, so to speak, in a state of stupefaction, a kind of permanent stupor, an irreparable silence, mouth open saying nothing and yet opening. And when I was a child, my mother used to say, "Close your mouth a bit when you're not talking. Keeping your mouth open like that makes you look like a moron." And I learned to close my mouth, to pinch my lips and lock my jaw. But I still forget sometimes.

JOAN IN HER FALL: My horse gallops with all his muscles
He is proud to be carrying an illiterate person
Because it is said that the word of God
Will be brought by the illiterate
My horse knows that he is carrying an illiterate person
Toward her mission
Ridding the country of the wicked
Of what is causing problems

I say to them
Go
Go crash somewhere else
There is no land of welcome
Search no longer it does not exist
Between the uterus and the tomb
We are doomed to wander eternally
Every land of welcome slips away from under our feet
Even the refuge of our thoughts is an illusion since God is everywhere
We will never be at peace
Never
My horse runs with all his strength
In the thick forest
Blue and yellow
His vision is panoramic
He can see as far as his own haunches
He sees big
His gaze enlarges what he gazes at
He sees the world as it is
Vague and uncertain
And suddenly my horse sees into the future
He sees the future
Then decides to drop
How to blame him
He drops everything
And it's the fall

JOAN'S MOTHER: Joan
Joan
She opened her eyes I'm not dreaming
Joan

Joan I'm your mother
Eat
Eat your meat
It's good for your health
It's horse meat

list inventory repertory stupefaction stupor broken amputated confession shame scandalized indignant answer spectacle mouth open closed pinch block forget potential possible limit hope habit reflex thought mystery sentence resistance oblique otherwise girl awakening memory walk forest hair mother hairdo teeth lips sky perfume deer coyote bird wild strawberry immortal flower goldenrod scratch cheek blood squirrel Aboriginal *Achillea millefolium* orange hawkweed fur cold ranunculus pungent yellow buttercup garlic vulnerable species excessive appetite too much all quest conquest error extent learn newborn nothing window fraction world design assemble discover matter ruin bulb knife bloom button bite smile root moss stream ravage ignorance memory loss sleep long time hope thin eyelid light flood violin nerve memory mute white strangeness aspect thing form intact father mother people animals room horse death force phenomenon theory principle law proof sense real uncertain morning time space oscillation relic possession greed lost common good heritage resource product treasure waste impermanence becoming patience usage language sponge withdraw rain cry window astonishment room aspect breached wall looking doctor nourish skinny porridge gruel salt sugar color starving vegetable tired leaf bitter nettle coal burning steak toothless fat whipped cream artichokes war bread pudding crumb French toast maple sap brandy rose water blood sausage orange blossom mother's milk champagne bubbles crab quail floating island couscous royal Maghreb swallow's nest Asia Arctic char you again wash slosh souvenir memory remain ruins grandiose catalogue census universe thing relation link weightlessness dispose grant part of the world event time movement language dog boy house bird patience given name age fall fold high horse fall night blood stain stone load suffering burden story walk look flower cat sun dangerous ocean origin sea eternal touch wet foam cold snow sweet dirty fragile food eat play vegetable meat horse health sleep eyes close tomorrow you rift soil jaw slip throat earth fall dream of fall somewhere nothing dead womb eyes mouth devour contain breath living flower memory voice something someone

JOAN IN THE APARTMENT: It's getting darker and darker
Men in grey suits
Are whispering and smoking
Around a bed
Where my father is dying relentlessly
My mother is serving them coffee
The apartment smells of church and shit
My father has almost rejoined his skeleton
Above the bed through the smoke
An image of Joan of Arc
Who declares that it is necessary to kick the enemy out of the country
To rip from the invader the holy soil of the homeland
And in a small frame can be read
Saint Joan of Arc Patron Saint and Protector of our Native Land
Thanks to your unending prayers may our country once more become Christian
And may it again find its unity
May it be
I look at my father
I promise him I will believe in nothing

I close my eyes on my father
And my father does not stop dying again and again inside my
  eyelids
I look at my father
His mouth is wide open and he is not speaking
He appears to not believe in his own death
I wish to say to him
I assure you that you are dead
I swear it to you
Believe me you are dead

4

The Language Of The Enemy

JOAN IN THE APARTMENT: One day, in catechism class, I was told that eternity is not just for always. It's also since always. That upset me. It's always, but going backward and going forward at the same time. That's infinity doubled. That's long. That means there is nothing else. There is nothing other than eternity. There is not another thing. It's disappointing. I'm going to follow you meekly, I promise you that, after all, why not, I'm even in a hurry, yes, I feel that I'll have no regrets, nothing, truly, I am at peace, you have calmed me, thank you, I'm going to follow you in the fullness of my heart, you'll see, but first . . . I would like . . . This is going to seem strange to you, but . . . I would like to offer you something of me. I mean I would like . . . I would like to be touched. There it is, take advantage of it.

She offers herself.

That leaves you speechless? I understand. Go ahead, don't be embarrassed. It's not a trap, it's quite simple and without ulterior motive. It's just because I want to be touched.

She offers herself once more.

You hesitate? You should take advantage of it. You won't get such an offer often.

DEATH remains cold. JOAN breaks down, humiliated.

You don't want to? Why? . . . But why? I know, I seem to be nothing, but I think I have great potential. You don't think so? That I have great potential?

JOAN'S MOTHER is pushing a baby carriage and speaking to her baby.

JOAN'S MOTHER: Can you see it, Joan? Here, it's the memory of a place that's been depleted. You can see the dead trees, you can see the broken windows, you can see that shell of an automobile, you can see the sheet metal, the plastic, the rubber. Can you see it? See it; take a good look. A part of the landscape must teach you of our inclination to sully and destroy. It's beautiful, isn't it?

JOAN IN HER FALL: We're lost.

JOAN'S MOTHER: We're not lost
What are you talking about
Stop crying
I tell you we're not lost

JOAN IN HER FALL: My mother thinks that I think that we are lost in the forest.

JOAN'S MOTHER: We're not lost
Look
There's a path
Paths are made to guide our steps

JOAN IN HER FALL: She shows me the path in order to show me we aren't lost.

JOAN'S MOTHER: Look!

JOAN IN HER FALL: She thinks that I think that we have lost our way, but I think that we are perishable and doomed.

JOAN'S MOTHER: Look at the beautiful path.

JOAN IN HER FALL: Every conversation with my mother is a misunderstanding.

JOAN'S MOTHER: It's beautiful isn't it
You love going for a walk in the forest with Mommy

JOAN IN HER FALL: I explain to my mother that we are all lost, in the forest just like everywhere else, because we are perishable, our ruins are predetermined, and soon we'll be corpses rotting and oozing liquids for the birds and insects to enjoy. And I cry.

> *JOAN'S MOTHER shakes the carriage to make the baby stop crying.*

JOAN'S MOTHER: Stop crying.

JOAN IN HER FALL: *(looking at the sky)* I don't stop crying.

JOAN'S MOTHER: *(also looking at the sky)* Stop!

JOAN IN HER FALL: I scream. All I know now is to scream.

JOAN'S MOTHER: Be quiet! Stop! Will you stop screaming!? My God, make her be quiet!

JOAN IN HER FALL: My mother thinks I'm teething
Just to let you know the extent of the misunderstanding
I look at the beautiful forest and my mother who is taking a walk there
Her steps sound like feathers
I look at my mother beautiful being in hair and skin
When I would like to see her meat and her bones
I open my eyes wider
I open my mouth
I open everything I can open
I open my hands my arms my thighs
I am a palm
All I am anymore is an open palm
Who is waiting
But nothing comes nothing comes nothing

She opens her mouth without making a sound.

JOAN'S MOTHER: Shut your mouth! Shut it! Shut it! Shut up!

JOAN IN THE APARTMENT: the alphabet in English magic realism Les Automatistes primary numbers elective affinities remarkable identities European capitals and the countries of Africa primary colours food groups leap years kings of France Galapagos Islands USSR parts of the eye Heimlich manoeuvre Higgs boson Laurentian flora the Age of Enlightenment Cuban Revolution Lac Léman One Hundred Years War Gulf War War of Secession Cold War Vietnam War Algerian War Mongol conquests September 2001 New Wave Gregorian chants American presidents martyrs saints famous criminals famous heroes famous geniuses famous suicides log drivers and patriots *The Little Mermaid* Émilie Jolie Phèdre Lady Macbeth the Pléiade Group of Seven existentialism Greek gods and their Roman equivalents fables of La Fontaine Venus de Milo *Prélude à l'après-midi d'un faune* and *The Rite of Spring L'origine du monde Les paradis artificiels The Crucible* Vestal Virgins Portuguese fados whirling dervishes Silver Factory Tea Party Beaver club Ku Klux Klan beatniks Beatles punks hipsters Khmers rouges Jimi Hendrix Lady Gaga Pina Bausch Stendhal syndrome Proust's madeleine Crohn's disease Plath's *Bell Jar* Pythagoras theorem Nagasaki Bloody Sunday Polytechnique *Charlie Hebdo* hanging gardens Garden of Earthly Delights Arab Spring Maple Spring minotaur chimera formula for the diameter periodic table traffic code Chinese astrological signs Lupus constellation national anthem the precise meaning of the words elegiac dialectic epigram innateness and demagogy past participles Mayakovsky "Le bateau ivre" "Only You" *Danton's Death* storming the Bastille World Cup Plains of Abraham oxymora hyperboles venial sins Three Wise Men greenhouse effect globalization baby's smell *La charge de l'orignal épormyable* Comtesse de Ségur drowned kitten *La nuit juste avant les forêts* Rue Blanche my first motorbike ride Étretat telephone announcement of Denis's death my wedding day 10th arrondissement Val-Morin stream when my mother was young connasse written in red on my locker *La maman et la putain Les bons débarras* my abortion *The Nutcracker The Wild Swans* and nettle knitting redemption of Jean Valjean and the dilemma of Javert Bérénice Einberg and her mother's hand Pope John Paul II in Parc Jarry "Une colombe est partie en voyage" Parc Belmont *Mommie Dearest L'effrontée* the last threat of the Old Testament three fishes on the catechism workbook *Cien años de soledad*

And in English? I often asked myself the question: What would have happened if I had been born in English, that language which I was taught is the language of the enemy, that language which attracted me among all the others precisely because it was the language of the enemy, and I tell myself that[5] maybe if I spoke English things would be different, maybe I would sound different in English, and maybe people would hear me better, maybe I would sound better speaking English, even if I don't know how, and I remember what I used to do when I was a child playing a Hollywood actress, hiding in my bedroom to speak the language of the enemy. I was looking at myself in the mirror to see if I was prettier when I spoke English. And something very strange happened: I was talking and suddenly I realized that I didn't understand what I was saying. I didn't understand a word. It felt good to hear myself without understanding anything. It sounded like music. Like water. No more misunderstanding. And I felt beautiful without any meaning. You hear? Would you touch me in English? Please?

DEATH: Sorry, I don't understand.

JOAN IN THE APARTMENT: Who are you?

DEATH: I am being about you.

JOAN IN THE APARTMENT: So, you are nobody? In my opinion hell is nobody. Nobody to touch you. In hell you freeze and there is nobody. In hell you die of loneliness and cold.

I begin again.

---

5 In the French staging, Joan In The Apartment slides into English at "maybe" and continues through "Who are you?" She returns to speaking French at the line "So, you are nobody?"

Everything would be different if we lived under our skeleton rather than over it. Everything would be different if we were made like shellfish and crustaceans. Skeleton outside. We would see our imminent death every day, in all the mirrors; we would have the time to get used to the idea; we would stop hoping for our soul to be saved. The problem is that we are put together inside out; we are decorative pieces it would be lovely to see overturned, so as to display our bones while scattering a bit of meat along the way; it would be an awesome upset—we would wear our skeleton like an ornament, like a trophy, like dazzling proof of our share in eternity, and then humanity on the march would be a parade of bones, a procession of fossils; we would take our skeleton for walks. It would smile with all its teeth as if to say to us that in the end there is nothing to fear, nor to hope.

It's so dark
Is anyone here
Can we do something about it
It's too dark
I'm not even asking for light
Just a glow
Barely a glimmer
Is anyone here

It begins to snow.

JOAN IN THE APARTMENT: It's snowing: a compromise between rain and batting, between matter and light.

DEATH: You must come with me, Joan.

JOAN IN THE APARTMENT: Already?

DEATH: Already.

JOAN IN THE APARTMENT: Oh.

DEATH: Yes.

He takes his coat and uses it to cover JOAN, *whom he embraces tenderly.*

Epilogue

Two Strangers[6]

Evening. A starry sky.

A YOUNG MAN*, alone. It is unclear to whom he is speaking, perhaps the sky.*

YOUNG MAN: Is anyone there?

An OLD MAN*, seeming to appear from nowhere, greets him.*

OLD MAN: Good evening.

YOUNG MAN: Oh, good evening. May I speak to you?

OLD MAN: Yes, of course.

YOUNG MAN: I live alone with my old mother, and our dog died today.

OLD MAN: Oh, I'm sorry.

YOUNG MAN: Usually, at this hour, I walk my dog.

OLD MAN: Yes, of course.

---

6 This epilogue was cut when the play was first staged. I chose to keep it for the publication, since it accompanied the entire gestation of the show (EdlC).

YOUNG MAN: I feel alone, walking alone this way.

OLD MAN: I understand.

YOUNG MAN: It's just a dog, but . . . it's hard.

OLD MAN: I understand.

YOUNG MAN: Ah, do you have a dog?

OLD MAN: No, but I have seen dying.

A long pause.

YOUNG MAN: The night is beautiful.

OLD MAN: Yes, it's a beautiful night.

They look at the stars.

YOUNG MAN: My mother asks to die and never does die.

OLD MAN: Does she have a good sense of humour?

YOUNG MAN: My mother?

OLD MAN: Yes.

YOUNG MAN: Yes. Yes, she has a good sense of humour. It seems to me that she has a good sense of humour.

OLD MAN: Well, that's good.

Beat.

YOUNG MAN: My mother's health has always been delicate, while our dog was in great shape.

OLD MAN: An accident?

YOUNG MAN: Yes.

OLD MAN: We all die alive.

They look at the stars again.

OLD MAN: There's going to be a lack of space, up there.

YOUNG MAN: Do you believe?

OLD MAN: In what?

The YOUNG MAN *does not catch the play on words—but is that what it truly is? In silence, they keep on looking at the sky.*

Afterword
by Louise H. Forsyth

Writing On A Wall

Playwright, actor, essayist, screen writer, and novelist Evelyne de la Chenelière responded with interest and enthusiasm after a short time of intense reflection to the invitation from Ginette Noiseux, Artistic and General Director at Espace GO in Montréal, to be artist-in-residence at the theatre for a three-year period (2014–2018). The residence proved to offer unique opportunities to explore and engage in dramaturgical, artistic, philosophical, and theoretical exploration and experimentation alone and with other artists. After several productive years of vibrantly rich creative involvement in theatrical and other live events, this moment was an opportune time for de la Chenelière to pause and reflect on what language, theatre, authenticity, and relationships meant to her, time to strike out in bold new directions despite and even because of the challenging uncertainty as to where these directions, not yet definitively formulated, could lead. De la Chenelière began this residency on August 13, 2014, when she climbed a small stepladder and made fresh red paint strokes on the wall of Espace GO's long café-bar hall. The strokes announced the intriguing title of what would underlie her project of mural writing, existential reflection, and dramaturgical exploration: "I'm starting over." ["Je recommence"].[1] This wall, upon

1 Citations and indications of page numbers from "Meandering and Shakes" are taken from the joint publication in French of this essay, "Errance et tremblements," and the play, *La vie utile* (Les Herbes Rouges,

which she wrote, painted, attached collages and other objects, and which came to display the characteristics of a vibrant and evolving palimpsest soon assumed its creative place as her "chantier d'écriture" (15), her "writing workshop," the place where she would undertake on an almost daily basis throughout the three-year residency a wide-ranging material and epistemological exploration of writing, theatricality, and the human condition with the intent of drawing out and refreshing the trembling energy of words by which it is possible to reach deeply into life.[2]

The objective of de la Chenelière's experimentation was to write words in fresh ways, particularly in writing theatre, with the goal of restoring untrammelled physicality and vitality to language and other representational forms. This objective entailed recognition of and resistance to clichés that can enter mindlessly onto theatrical stages, reflecting and reinforcing thereby hackneyed repetitions in form and content occurring in dramaturgical practice and in everyday language usage in theatre and society generally. De la Chenelière attributed these same reservations regarding words and language to Joan In The Apartment

2019). Translations of these citations, done by LHF, are from the present publication.

2 De la Chenelière's work on the Espace GO café-bar wall did not have and was not intended to have a permanent place in the theatre. Nevertheless, the wall functioned as an artistic, conceptual, and virtual field inviting the artist herself and all those who passed before it onto time-space paths only dreams, fantasies, memories, and imaginations can summon. Her work on the wall was removed following the residency, but not before it was photographed and preserved as photographic archives at Espace GO. These archives also contain reproductions of works by other artists who engaged in creative response to and dialogue with the wall in the course of de la Chenelière's residency. They are likely to evoke particularly powerful and challenging visual resonance for readers and spectators of *Ravage of Life* and will undoubtedly stir stimulating trembles and shakes in those who undertake a production of the play in English.

by which, in a monologue, she launches *Ravage of Life*, while declaring and repeating that she is starting over:

> As soon as I was taught that it takes words to designate the world and all we think of it, communication using language came to seem very complicated to me and quite ambitious. I said to myself that people who claim that they're able to say what they're thinking must not think very much, because language is without the power to convey the boundlessness of living thought, its interruptions, its eternal returns, its incessant convulsions. [. . .] In fact, I have always found that language gives credibility and certainty to what only seems real. Language is without the power to adapt to the world as I perceive it: turbid, uncertain, changing. (62)

De la Chenelière expressed this objective in the first paragraph of "Toward *Ravage of Life*," Part Two of "Meandering and Shakes," focusing on her extraordinary approach to the play as she and Marie Brassard moved collaboratively toward its stage creation. This objective, which she chose for her entire residency period, was to make theatre that differs in major ways from prevailing norms of theatre practice. She saw the theatre around her and perhaps even her own thus far as determined by institutionalized conventions that left much that is vibrant and vital unspoken and unacknowledged. This radical objective, focusing particularly on moving outside of received languages of theatrical creation, left her with a desire to transgress the rules in place and so to "open up signs, try to eviscerate theatre. Make theatre the place where thought finds its body. Dig into the space that exists between the parts of a sentence. [. . .] Free oneself from a grammar that binds like a spell, that limits the will to think" (45).

Like graffiti and other forms of public art, de la Chenelière's writing on the theatre's café-bar wall can be seen as a unique personal statement of artistic agency, resistance, and protest meant to evoke reactions, responses, and to encourage others to provide their own creative perspectives on the issues raised, whatever their medium and particular artistic approach might be.

De la Chenelière formulated her plan for the residency and the strategies arising from this plan before she accepted Noiseux's residency offer: "Before making a commitment I felt it was important to look within myself for an approach that would allow me to enhance this residency but also remain tuned into my own deepest and most vital concerns. Above all, I had to find the drive [. . .]" (11).

The details of this plan, bearing particularly on her approach to the work she would be doing in her residency and in the play she would write were displayed on the wall early in her work. The eleven points of the plan, all beginning with "I wish to [. . .]," constitute an *ars poetica* indicating her strategies by which she plans to escape from forms grown hackneyed through habit and facile conformity to prevailing norms. She intended to explore that which can only be glimpsed beyond words by meandering through intervals in quiet non-verbal messages accessed while trembling and wandering.

The points of her plan (13–15), which underlie and illuminate the creative process leading to and resulting in *Ravage of Life*, were reproduced on the wall almost entirely unchanged three years after their initial formulation as given in "Meandering and Shakes." They express de la Chenelière's powerful and sustained resistance to unchanging and authoritative norms and traditions for making theatre, the existence of which stifles the force of independent thought and vibrant sensitivity while concealing the creative impulse of writing as focused work and bold engagement.

The photos of the wall kept in the archives show de la Chenelière's final addition to the eleven points of her initial plan: "So I propose to write in the hall of Espace GO on supports that make writing visible."

With the compelling energy emerging from de la Chenelière's own experimental initiatives, as well as the rich mosaic of voices and visions arising from other artists' collaboration in their response to her invitation and her work, the stages and various other spaces of Espace GO took on their own dynamic air for three years with extraordinary forms, words, sounds, actions, ideas, and objects. The writing on the wall, along with a rich gamut of performances, multidisciplinary activities, talks, installations, spontaneous encounters among artists and spectators, wove the fabric of a context nurturing her co-authorship in 2016 with Justin Laramée of the dramatic text *Nous reprendrons tout ça demain* ["We'll pick all that back up tomorrow"].[3] The end of de la Chenelière's artistic residency was marked by the staging

3 Joan's Mother says this in *La vie utile* (72) to the young Joan when tucking her into bed after a final training session on proper language usage and manners. Justin Laramée adopted this statement as the title of his play. His collaboration with de la Chenelière in creating *Nous reprendrons tout ça demain* is among the first dialogic responses from an artist to her writing on the wall. He said about their collaboration and the powerful impact on him of the play in "Mise en contexte. Un mur qui deviendra une pièce" ["Contextualisation. A Wall That Will Become a Play"]: "Je devais lier le geste d'Evelyne, l'incidence qu'il avait sur moi, aux traces qui me parvenaient, distillées de son environnement, de ses mots. [. . .] Le texte qui suit relève de l'architecture: le matériau (les mots, les phrases) sont d'Évelyne et la structure (les scènes, les personnages, la construction dramaturgique) sont de moi" [I needed to link Évelyne's action, its effect on me, to the traces that came to me, distilled from her environment, from her words. The text of [*Nous reprendrons*] lies in the realm of architecture: the raw material (the words, the sentences) are by Evelyne and the structure (the scenes, the characters, the dramaturgical shape) by me] (11). *Nous reprendrons* received a dramatic reading at Espace GO on September 16, 2016.

at Espace GO of *La vie utile*, directed by Marie Brassard, which opened April 24, 2018. De la Chenelière played the role of Joan In The Apartment in this premiere of the play.

De la Chenelière chose to place her essay "Errance et tremblements" before *La vie utile* in the publication of her play. In publishing the essay after her artistic residency, she is indicating that her wrap-up publication is looking back in order to provide a retroactive look at the work she did on the wall while writing *La vie utile*.

The quotation from philosopher Giorgio Agamben's *Il fuoco e il racconto*, standing as an epigraph at the start of "Meandering and Shakes," raises some of the questions that determined the shape of de la Chenelière's work on the wall and in *Ravage of Life*. These questions set the direction for her work throughout the residency with regard to what words can and cannot do and what in reality eludes the reach of words alone, the moral and ethical problematics of language usage and discourse, epistemologically driven awareness of realities that can be sensed yet are neither effable nor conceptually accessible, the power of poetry in providing access to this realm of what cannot be said and yet can be felt and recognized for its vibrant reality. De la Chenelière formulated in "Meandering and Shakes" her discomfort with familiar and seemingly normal discursive patterns that create the impression common cultural and verbal norms, widely accepted and adopted, provide a grasp on known and unassailable truths and realities. Yet the very familiarity and habitual nature of these norms, the complacent comfort one feels in adhering to them, is an indication of their facile capacity to deceive, to nurture hastily adopted errors and misconceptions, to encourage individuals to remain on the surface of their perceptions. The clichés spontaneously reinforced by that which is familiar through habit dull the sharpness of full sensitivity and obstruct access to the ineffable, which she senses in words and verbal expressions that are free to wander poetically unhindered in free-floating semiotic spheres. Her view, as expressed in "Meandering and Shakes," is that words as commonly written and spoken have been frozen into fixed form and meaning through institutionally and culturally sanctioned repetitions reinforced by comfortable familiarity. They are erroneously taken to be reliable avenues into the world's and one's own reality. Such discursive patterns lend themselves to abuse of power and nurture the conformity and complacency that come with the facile adoption of dominant forms. These forms foreclose in advance entrance into the complex depths that poetry can open, at least partially, if one allows oneself to drift on its tremulous lines.

Profoundly concerned about the loss of freedom of thought, the constraints placed on imagination, the dulling of sensitivity, and the banality of beliefs and attitudes that remain stalled in the commonplace, de la Chenelière asks: "What room is left for attention, anxiety, doubt, desire, ambiguity, mystery, opacity, uncertainty? Is there still a vacant space to commit to? Where? How? Why? For whom? Where is genuine resistance to be found?" (12). Effective responses to these compelling questions come by taking a break, moving into conceptual exile so as to begin anew and re-establish ties through poetic expression with a state that predates the seemingly inevitable acquisition in every individual of formulaic discursive, perceptual, and conceptual habits and that lends itself to vibrating with the dynamic force of words, a force that surpasses in its sounds, shapes, rhythms, associations, complexities, and intensities their primary meanings and that serves to launch richer awareness. This exile, which weaves like a time-space gap throughout "Meandering and Shakes," is titled "Interval," an "an irreplaceable, autonomous, full instant" (43) that can be accessed for the fullness of untrammelled perception by receptive and sensitive individuals who have rid themselves of the dulling impact of habit and convention.

In this state of detachment reached through processes of unlearning received meanings, ideas, memories, and beliefs, imagination can be renewed, buried memory can be excavated and brought to light: "In order to reach that fantastical idea of *re-commencement*, which requires a total reconfiguration of what is real, I projected myself into radical unlearning based on memory and forgetting" (16–17).[4]

De la Chenelière's determination to adopt an approach to writing with a starting point in rupture and exile entailed not only free play with the meanings, sounds, and forms of words, but also with their functions in grammatical or generic structures and their material substance. The condition of exile she chose to be hers as a writer on the wall required that she transform her relation to her body and that she abandon certain writing habits for this project. This led her to reject paper, on which she had always written until then, and to move into the space where she literally painted letters with a brush directly on the wall. This resulted in the construction over the three-year period of the large three-layered palimpsest. This action, which she termed *écrire par le corps* [*writing with the body*] (21), opened new dimensions and structures for words and transported them into different patterns and forms, to the point of their being literally tangible. Producing these words, and the images that accompanied them, required sustained corporeal

4 De la Chenelière resists the search for commercial success or artistic perfection as determined by traditionally institutionalized standards for their way of limiting freedom and rendering authentic perception and expression inaccessible. Leonard Cohen expresses the same awareness of an ineffable beyond in "Anthem" (1992): "Ring the bells that still can ring / Forget your perfect offering / There is a crack in everything / That's how the light gets in."

adaptation and frequent use of devices to obtain appropriate access to the wall's surface. Each day every part of her body was obliged to adjust to the needs for writing on the wall at that particular moment:

> The physical commitment required for the action of writing on a wall was a way for me to make the meaning of my commitment to creation visible and tangible. I felt that I was *writing writing*—that is to say tracing it, painting it, sticking it, making it material, indeed, an excess transcending thought itself. Writing while standing, lying down, perching, taking the chance that a body invested in writing can rip language right out of its own system of alienation, trivialization, subjection. As if only the body could restore the strangeness of words, separate them from every value established by verbal habits. [. . .] I had the feeling at the sight of this work of digging into trembling form, its infinite potential, its readiness. [. . .] Thus, in the course of days and layers, to the beat of my thrusts and retractions, the palimpsest wall became the palpitating, unstated, and dogged embryo of a thing which, still today, I could not comprehend exactly. (20–21)

The living force hovering in words can be released when thought rips itself free from timeworn patterns and moves into "a kind of living radiation pursuing an invisible and unfathomable trajectory" (35). Moving with such radiation offers the thrill of shifting into previously unknown time-space dimensions in both self and the world. This inspiration accompanied de la Chenelière in the process of writing *Ravage of Life* and determined her theoretical and aesthetic objectives for the play.

From The Wall To The Stage

In the second part of "Meandering and Shakes," "Toward *Ravage of Life*," de la Chenelière sketched this process. Having explored in the first part of the essay her approach to writing, language, and discourse and recalled significant moments on her path as a writer moved by the radical objective of boldly and freely reaching out to life regardless of dominant trends that may not lend themselves to such an objective, she turned specifically in this second part of the essay to her aims as a writer of theatre. This entailed moving into a sort of conceptual exile and unlearning the dictates of convention, tradition, and habit when it comes to the elements of what is generally deemed to be a good play. For readers and spectators of the play, this radical approach can be quite disconcerting, since it involved rethinking the generic norms for theatre in script writing and theatrical practices in representation of place, time, characterization, story, relations among characters, action, dialogue, plot, denouement, and thematic development. The titles of the six sections in this part of the essay provide an introductory outline from both a creative and practical perspective on the exploratory journey she took in her move between writing on the Espace GO wall and *writing Ravage of Life* for the stage: "Induce Writing," "From the Wall to the Stage," "The Dead and the Living," "What Could Be Read on Stage," "Joan and Joan of Arc," "Looking Back."

De la Chenelière devoted the first section of "Toward *Ravage of Life*," "Induce Writing," to a fundamental and essential part of her residency, that of inducing writing beyond herself through sharing with other artists, all of whom she encouraged to respond in their own way and in their own artistic discipline to her work on the wall. She provides a list of thirteen artists whom she invited to *write* their own original work in their discipline in response to what her text said to them. The impact on her wall and her theatre writing of the representation of their "intimate and secret relation" with the wall through their own unique perspective was to bring the shakes of her words out into the light: "[. . .] thanks to their ways of seeing that convert reality, ways of seeing that are fertile and inspired looking at the wall, they pulverized it, made it burst open, gutted it, unfolded it infinitely to the point where it opens beyond itself. A bird overreaching its own wingspan" (46–47).

These were steps in the spontaneous and energetic project I have already discussed regarding de la Chenelière's writing collaboration with Justin Laramée. Brassard, like Laramée, was one of the artists invited by de la Chenelière to engage in dialogue with her wall. De la Chenelière felt in Brassard a kindred creative spirit sensitive to the rich evocative power of words freed from mindless habit to explore the limitless ranges of vision made available in poetic languages and on theatre stages: "If I am a writer *for* the stage, she is a writer *of* the stage; I was convinced that the intermingling of what we wrote would bring a surprising, free, and unusual work" (47). Together, in their shared search for theatrical renewal, they addressed questions that were both theoretical and practical. These questions and their joint vision of how best to address them in actual performance led to a play text that departed from all conventional norms:

> Is there a form other than language to embrace the limitlessness of living thought? How is it possible for time to unfold differently on stage? How can the stage be turned into a territory where nothing sets or becomes immobile, and where each step, gesture, wave, and shock modifies its contours? How can the stage suggest a place beyond place, out of the box, beyond norm and beyond time, a place where, simply, something is taking shape? (48)

Knowing that their approaches to writing and creating for theatre were congenial and that they both identified with much that was written on the wall, Brassard and de la Chenelière worked closely together in their wish "to bring to light the limitless nature of what we can see and understand in that which surrounds us, contains us, maintains us, survives us" (48).

De la Chenelière continued in the third section of the essay, "The Dead and the Living," to take radical steps in her probe and broad revisioning of conventions involved in theatrical creation. At first glance *Ravage of Life* appears to fit comfortably into the mould of bourgeois drama. Its characters conform to the model of the average family: mother, father, and children. However, the long opening monologue of Joan In The Apartment does not address any theme normally associated with what is called bourgeois theatre. Instead, she introduces topics associated with metaphysical questioning and human mortality such as faith, death, the afterlife, language, and social values. The monologue is interrupted by the disconcerting words of Joan's Father, who launches into the eternity of Joan's fall to the entrails of the earth. Joan's Mother and Joan In Her Fall then speak from another location on stage, each proceeding in her own space on her own timeline through her own story. From that starting moment in the play spectators and readers are likely to feel tension and disconnection among the four characters, due to the absence of a logical storyline and disparity among the themes, perceptions, events, and life moments in which they are engaged, due as well to the absence of links among their experiences. Death soon arises in each of their lives in one form or another. While these various and disparate elements of the family's stories do not ever come together to form a coherent and logical series of events, not even at the play's conclusion, de la Chenelière indicates in the fourth section, contrary to any logical interpretation, that these events all occur *at the same time* while words drawn from the play outside of syntax fall like snowflakes (50). De la Chenelière leaves readers, audience members, and spectators free to move out of their box in order to use their own imagination and creative force to bring for themselves coherence and meaning to the whole of the play.

In line with her resistance to claims for discursive infallibility when it comes to the use of words, as is invariably claimed for the Bible and Grevisse's grammatical rules, de la Chenelière has chosen not to provide readers or spectators any clear statement regarding what the show or the experiences of the characters mean. One notes, in this regard, that *Ravage of Life* is almost completely devoid of stage directions and any form of didascalia. The words spoken by the characters indicate throughout the play that they are most often not together in the same place nor at the same time as the others. Their snippets of conversation come and go, sometimes with thematic connection, but receivers are left to fit them together on their own using their own imagination, dreams, and devices. Indeed, even the dead and the absent have their place in the exchanges on stage. Without clear indication from de la Chenelière's text, directors, designers, and actors are free to construct the disparate elements of space as best serves their interpretation of events, words, and actions on stage. Only the window on stage appears to have a particular significance in its representation of, on the one hand, an opportunity to see out, for purposes of perception of what might be real out there and, on the other, the control and limitation of how much can be seen, imposed by an object such as the window, which always has hard edges closing off what lies beyond.

Further to these gaps in what is normally seen on stage as part of a coherent whole, there is also de la Chenelière's use of language, which departs in a radical way from discursive conventions and grammatical rules. Rather than organizing words in the normal linear order of prose writing, she has chosen in several places to organize them in accordance with the conventions of musical notation, which is built, through vertical structure, on the performance of multiple voices, harmonies, disharmonies, simultaneity, disparate rhythms.

De la Chenelière indicates that words, powerful repositories of meaning and sound, have the potential to play in many different ways when they are released from the constraints of stereotypes, grammatical structure, fixed context, and form. This almost limitless virtuality of words when free to exercise their entire range is eloquently dramatized on various occasions in *Ravage of Life* when words come fluttering down like unnamed snowflakes to be gathered and used by whoever claims them (75–76, 85, 96–97, 107–08, 114–15, 120–22).

The fourth section of the essay sees the arrival of death in the lives of all the characters, other than Death himself and Joan's Mother. The action shifts rapidly from one site to the next. Death arrives while Joan In The Apartment is busy with housework. Joan In Her Fall dies in a fall from her horse, dreams of Joan Of Arc, and watches her father die. Joan's Father appears to speak from the beyond; Joan's Mother teaches conformity to a young Joan by showing her the way to stay on the right paths in the natural world, while tirelessly repeating the requirement that her daughter watch: "Look!"

In the end they all fade away, stripped of their theatrical existence with no definitive responses in their various quests, as is appropriate in what de la Chenelière termed a "theatre of erosion" (49). Makers and receivers of the play are left with the many disparate elements of the show to claim, put together, and work out for themselves in ways and modes that work best for them in any desire they might have for coherence and meaning (48–49).

Making no claims for either transcendent meaning or rational coherence, all the better to favour sensation, emotion, creativity, and living thought, de la Chenelière states her objective as a writer for theatre in terms of reaching for freedom, authenticity, complicity with other creative seekers in lives they are patching together in the same way as she:

> The time of dying becomes eternity; eternity of an imbalance—imbalance of the stance of doubt, eternity of uncertainty in the face of origin as of becoming, eternity of seeking to discover what it's all about. My writing seeks to stage the anarchic reconstitution of the past and the building of a potential and uncertain future. It turns memory into spectacle. (49)

Acknowledgements

The author would like to warmly thank Sylvain Lavoie.

About the Author

Writer and actress Evelyne de la Chenelière is an essential figure within Québec theatre. Translated and presented throughout the world, her plays question the limits of language and the experience of writing. In 2017 she was a finalist for the Siminovich Prize for excellence and innovation in Canadian theatre. Among her works, *La vie utile*, created at Espace GO and staged at the Festival TransAmériques, received the Marcel Dubé Award from the Académie des lettres du Québec, and premiered in German in Frankfurt. *Bashir Lazhar* was adapted into the film *Monsieur Lazhar* by Philippe Falardeau and was nominated for an Academy Award for Best Foreign Language Film. Her most recent play, *Le traitement de la nuit*, was directed by Denis Marleau in Montréal, premiered in Frankfurt in German translation, and was the subject of a public reading at the Comédie Française in Paris. Evelyne de la Chenelière's journey is marked by formal exploration and a desire to question living art, both through writing and acting. A singular artist who defies expectations, her work is present in major institutions in Québec and abroad, but also lives within their hidden margins.

About the Translator

Louise H. Forsyth (1935–2024) was a trailblazing academic who specialized in French Canadian literature and taught drama, poetry, and women's and gender studies at Western University and the University of Saskatchewan. She was a founding member of the Canadian Association for Theatre Research and held several administrative positions throughout her career. Her many published articles, books, translations, and scholarly papers on Québec women playwrights and poets includes the three-volume *Anthology of Québec Women's Plays in English Translation*, Marie Savard's *Bien à moi* (*Mine Sincerely*), *Nicole Brossard: Essays on her Works*, and *Mobility of Light: The Poetry of Nicole Brossard.*

First edition: August 2024
Printed and bound in Canada by Imprimerie Gauvin Ltée, Gatineau

Jacket art by Evelyne de la Chenelière, photograph by Marlène Gélineau Payette
Photos by Marlène Gélineau Payette (inside cover, 9, 11, 17, 21, 27), Hubert Larose St-Jacques (32–33), and David Ospina (42–43, 50–51, 52–53)

Playwrights Canada Press
202-269 Richmond St. W., Toronto, ON M5V 1X1
416.703.0013 | info@playwrightscanada.com | www.playwrightscanada.com

LIBRARY AND ARCHIVES CANADA CATALOGUING IN PUBLICATION
Title: Ravage of life / Evelyne de la Chenelière ; translated by Louise H. Forsyth.
Other titles: La vie utile. English
Names: De la Chenelière, Evelyne, 1975- author. | Forsyth, Louise H., translator.
Description: Translation of: La vie utile. | Includes bibliographical references.
Identifiers: Canadiana (print) 20230540643 | Canadiana (ebook) 20230540767
| ISBN 9780369102720 (softcover) | ISBN 9780369102737 (PDF)
| ISBN 9780369102744 (EPUB)
Classification: LCC PS8555.H44526 V5413 2023 | DDC C842/.6—dc23

Playwrights Canada Press operates on land which is the current and ancestral home of the Anishinaabe Nations (Ojibwe / Chippewa, Odawa, Potawatomi, Algonquin, Saulteaux, Nipissing, and Mississauga), the Wendat, and the members of the Haudenosaunee Confederacy (Mohawk, Oneida, Onondaga, Cayuga, Seneca, and Tuscarora), as well as Metis and Inuit peoples. It always was and always will be Indigenous land.

We acknowledge the financial support of the Canada Council for the Arts, the Ontario Arts Council (OAC), Ontario Creates, the Government of Ontario, and the Government of Canada for our publishing activities.